VALERIE L. HARRIS

COURAGE TO HEAL
AND TO LET GO

© 2024 by Valerie Harris
Published by: **DR75** / Stefan Heikens
Edited by: Nicole Niehoff
Herstellung und Verlag:
BoD - Books on Demand, Norderstedt (GER)
ISBN: 9783758372612

DEDICATION

WILLIE E. HARRIS – My life partner, my beloved husband, my best friend in life. Thank you for not giving up on me. I love you!

MATTHEW – You are the gift God gave to me in my darkest hours. I wouldn't have a story to share with others without you.

CHARLOTTE, SONDRA, JOHN – I cherish everything about you. My life would be incomplete without you and I could not love you any more than I do right now.

MARCUS – Stay close to the fire of God and trust his plan for your life. You have a story of your own to tell that will change the heart of many.

<u>CONTENTS</u>

CHAPTER

POEM

FOREWORD

As you begin to read this book, I would like for you to take a journey with me. The purpose of me writing this book is to perhaps help someone on their journey called life. One thing that I've learned and lived is that the road is not always easy, but there is hope and there is healing for a wounded heart. No matter the age, no matter the situation, no matter the pain or the struggle, you are not alone. For the purpose of transparency and truth, I share segments of my own life with the intent to touch and encourage you to find it within yourself to love, to forgive, and most of all, the courage to heal and to let go. There truly is a light that will shine through the darkness. I chose not to use names because there may be those in your own journey whom you may relate to. However, the characters are real. The names aren't as important as the experience of the journey. If you see yourself within these pages, you can inject the character or person who has affected your own life and your own journey. If sharing my story would help at least one person, then my labor would not have been in vain. May your eyes be opened to see the victor come forth, and to put the victim to rest. There are so many people who are hurting for so many different reasons, but life also provides the answer. You will find that you are stronger than you think and you are not alone. God has a plan and a purpose for your life and I truly believe that you will prevail and become all that you were meant to be. There is a bright Light that shines in the darkness. Be encouraged and may your very soul be filled with the Light of God's eternal love. This is personal. I know that I am not alone so I pray that you or someone you know will have the Courage to Heal and to Let Go.

Love, Valerie

CHAPTER 1

I HEARD HIS VOICE

The LORD is my shepherd; I shall not want. He makes me to lie down in green pastures; He leads me beside the still waters. He restores my soul; He leads me in the paths of righteousness for His name's sake. Yea though I walk through the valley of the shadow of death, I will fear no evil; for You are with me; Your rod and Your staff, they comfort me. You have prepared a table before me in the presence of my enemies; You anoint my head with oil; My cup runs over. Surely goodness and mercy shall follow me all the days of my life; and I will dwell in the house of the Lord Forever.

"But you will not die."

I heard His voice so clearly as I was laying naked on a bed and this man was on top of me, raping me. I just knew I would never see my family again. I was going to die. His friend must have grown tired because I had been there all night while the two of them raped me and at one point they were both inside of me at the same time. When would this nightmare end? In the quietness of my thoughts, in my silence, I had begun to recite the words of Psalm 23 for they would be my last words, my last thoughts. I was numb and I could not feel my body. It was the only prayer I had learned, besides the Lord's prayer which my mother taught me when I was a little girl.

I picked up one of her books one day and I read Psalm 23. The words were so beautiful that I remembered them. I didn't understand its meaning, but apparently, it became a part of me. I don't recall reciting it until this moment when I believed my life was over. I can honestly say that I did not know God at the time but I was searching for Him.

When I was ten years old, my niece, my nephew and I attended Summer Vacation Bible School at this church down the street from where my sister lived. It was fun. We learned some songs, learned the books of the Bible, played games and had snacks. I was talking to a school friend on the phone and she asked me if I had been baptized. When my response was "No," she told me I was going to Hell if I didn't get baptized. I didn't even know what Hell was, but she scared me to death. When the preacher asked if anyone wanted to be baptized, I was a candidate.

On Sunday morning he called me to come forth for baptism. We were standing in the baptism pool and he instructed me to hold my breath, which I did. Then he started speaking to the congregation. He had talked so long that I tried to take another breath and he dunked me in the water. While I was under the water I could hear him say, "I baptize you in the name of the Father, the Son, and the Holy Ghost". He seemed to drag these words out and I was thinking, "This man is trying to drown me!" This experience scared me so bad that I didn't go back. Occasionally I'd attend church with my dad. The church would be full and I just didn't get it. I would generally fall asleep. I had opened the Bible before but after the first line, I was so bored that I couldn't keep my eyes open. I was Bible illiterate.

When I was 21-years-old, one of my college friends invited me to church. It was close to campus. I don't remember the message but it caused me to be curious about "Who is God?" I graduated from college six months earlier than expected and when I returned home I began to ask people "What is the gospel?" The response would always be "The Good News." Well, "What is the good news?" I would ask, but no one gave me an answer that would appease me. I was 21 years old and I knew nothing about living. I knew of God, but I didn't know anything about God. Yet in the darkest moment of my life, "**He spoke to me**." My body was there on the bed, but the rest of me was not. I could not speak a word. There were no more tears for me to shed. I was completely numb and empty.

When this rapist had enough, he instructed me to get dressed and he said he would take me home. Daybreak was already on the horizon this Sunday morning. As I was getting dressed, this voice guided me to look around the room and the rest of the apartment and remember what I saw. I had no emotions but I was completely focused. I didn't speak but I followed the instructions that were given to me through this voice and I began to memorize my surroundings.

When I got to this man's car I looked at the license plate, outside the car, inside the car, and the outer surroundings. He actually stopped at a convenience store to get gas. He had to go into the store and I didn't move. I was so focused on the details, it never dawned on me to get out of the car and run. He drove me to an area which I knew. I told him to let me out on the corner and he did. He left and I began to walk home. I was quite a distance away from home and a car pulled up and the driver asked me if I needed a ride.

I got in the car with this stranger and I just stared out of the window as he was taking me home. I never looked at him. He asked me if I was okay and as silent tears began to fall, I told him that I had just been raped. He was at a loss for words. The only conversation we had was concerning the directions to my house. He dropped me off in my driveway and I thanked him. I was literally still numb. I never looked at this man who brought me home. I never saw his face or asked for his name nor did he ask for mine. I hadn't thought about how foolish and naive it was for me to get into the car with a strange man. But I have to believe that it was God who prompted him to help me. He truly could have been an angel. He was mine that day and I did tell him "Thank you."

I went to the back door of the house because my keys and my purse were not with me. My sister and I had gone to a club the night before and were separated, so she had my things. She opened the door for me and I immediately asked her for pen and paper. I sat at the kitchen table and I jotted down everything that I had memorized. Just as I finished, I fell apart and began to cry. I briefly told my sister what happened and my mother walked through the door. She had gone to work but she was so worried about me, she came back home. I was so ashamed that I could not look at her.

My sister got dressed and took me to *Ben Taub Hospital*. *Ben Taub* was the county hospital. I was still in the same clothes. It was a one piece orange jumpsuit. Usually, this hospital is so full, especially on the weekend. Generally you would have to wait hours to be seen but they saw me almost immediately. I was still numb – in a daze. When the doctor came back in the room, he said he would give me a shot to prevent a venereal disease and he informed me that I was pregnant. He asked me if I wanted an abortion and I said "No." I never had the thought that this baby was a product of the rape. I was on birth control pills and was sexually involved with my boyfriend so I didn't ask any questions, nor did I have any doubt. It appeared that everything within me had completely stopped. In that moment I realized there was a life inside of me. I was still quite numb but the innocent life on the inside of me somehow gave me a reason to live. In the midst of all of this darkness and confusion, God had given me a gift – a gift of life. In an instant, I fell in love with this unborn child and I just knew I had to protect him.

After speaking to the police, I was given the instruction to come to the police station and to bring all of the clothes I was wearing with me. Just then, my boyfriend walked into the room and wanted to know the details of what happened to me and I told him. He never wanted to hear it again. What I hadn't shared was that on the darkest day of my life – when I just knew I was going to die – God rescued me. **I heard His Voice.**

WHEN YOU CALL

When You call, 'O Lord, I will answer
There is no greater treasure than my fellowship with You
You have fearfully and wonderfully created me from Your substance
And it is Your breath that sustains my life
There is absolutely nothing that I can do apart from You
There is no place I may go where I go alone
No words spoken by man, nor songs composed
Can compare with Your Voice when You speak to my heart
Your Word is the mirror that shows me – me.
Whether good or bad, I bring all that I am to You
Yielded and surrendered
My life to be emptied of self and selfish desires
To be filled and consumed by Your Spirit
In Your sanctuary, I will reverence You
And before Your altar, I will give You praise
Your temple is Holy
And in Your place, You are highly exalted and greatly honored
I worship at Your feet and I bless Your name.
Lord, when You call, I will answer.

CHAPTER 2

FORBIDDEN FRUIT

I had this vivid memory of a dream that I had the night before my sister and I went to the club. I was sitting at the kitchen table sharing with my mom, telling her the details of what happened to me and I remembered the dream. It was clear as day. In the dream I saw the rape. In the dream I saw that I was pregnant. In the dream I knew that it was a boy. What I didn't understand was why didn't I remember the dream until after these events happened? Was God giving me a warning and I didn't listen? Or was it a part of my destiny? My mind was boggled. I blamed myself for being so naive. It seemed so unreal. Somehow the worst day of my life became the best day of my life because I heard God's voice and I had discovered the gift of life on the inside of me. It shouldn't make sense but this child in my womb saved me and this horrible event would redirect the course of my life. I had hope. I had to survive for him. I wouldn't trade anything for my journey. This statement is more than a cliché because of the reality that God is truly real and He not only spared my life, He changed my life.

It's somewhat crazy when I think about how the fragments of my memories began to flood my mind and to shape my life. I may not have understood it at the time, but my whole entire life was about to take a turn.

I remember a day when I was on the playground at school. It was quite a fun day with a Maypole and all. I couldn't have been more than five or six-years-old. I was in elementary school and I was walking home from school that day with the boy who lived on the corner. When we reached his house, he told me about the plum tree in his backyard and asked me if I wanted some

17

plums. I immediately said yes. We had pear trees in our backyard, but I had never seen a plum tree. We walked into his backyard and he told me I had to give him my panties for the plums. I paused and pondered the strange request for a moment, but I wanted those plums. Well, back then we didn't have those conversations. No one had ever told me that it was wrong. You found out it was wrong when you messed up and there were consequences for your actions.

As I think about it now, I can only imagine Eve being alone in the garden with the serpent. When she saw that the fruit was appealing to the eye, she was mesmerized by the fruit. When she and Adam ate the forbidden fruit they were put out of the garden and sin had fallen upon all humanity.

I strolled home with my plums and when my mom discovered that I had traded my panties for some plums, I got the whooping of my life! So when a family member started molesting me, I was too afraid to tell anyone. I suffered in silence. I began to have nightmares. Every night my dreams would be of me at school where a huge black hole would open up and I would fall in. I could literally feel myself falling but I would always wake up before I hit the bottom. I would wake up in a dark room and I was terrified. I couldn't wait until morning came. I remember sitting on the curb in front of our house, watching the cars go by and pondering which car I would run in front of. I did not want to be there. I just wanted to disappear and die.

It didn't happen every day. Every day wasn't a bad day. I had some really good days, as well. Our community was close. Everyone looked out for one another and the kids were allowed to play in the streets until the daylight was gone. As soon as you saw the sun going down, you'd better be in the house.

———

Our next door neighbor would round us up and take us to the park to play baseball so we wouldn't break any car or house windows. We still would gather together and play in the streets too. We jumped ropes, played hide and seek, Simon Says, hopscotch, climbed trees, played football, skating, jacks, racing – anything we could imagine. We just had fun. Sometimes I would just lay in the driveway and look into the sun all by myself and daydream. Of course, our chores had to be done and our homework had to be done before we were allowed to play outside. My sister and I shared a bedroom and I was fortunate to have the bed by the window.

I loved reading. I was in the 3rd grade and I was reading "*The Goose That Laid The Golden Egg*." I was so focused on the book that I did not hear my teacher talking to me. She came up behind me with her paddle board and struck me across my back, demanding that I put the book away and pay attention. I was so afraid of this woman. I actually thought she was a witch. When we were promoted to another grade we kept the same teacher in elementary school. This time during our math session, I was reading "*Henny Penny*." She knew I wasn't paying attention to the math on the board so she called me to answer the problem. I was certain that she was trying to embarrass me before the entire class. I looked up and blurted out the answer – which, by the way, was the correct answer. It was at that point that I obtained a fear of reading, and math became my favorite subject.

One night I was looking out of my window and the sky was filled with bright starry lights. I was so captured and in awe of this beautiful night sky. These words came to me. "*The stars that shine are in the night. The stars they shine with beauty so bright. The stars they shine with hope and fear. And bring us great happiness from far and near.*" I took to pen and paper and titled my very first poem "*The Stars.*" I was too young to realize that this was a gift. For me, it was healing. It was actually the only poem I've ever written that I remember the words. I finally had a voice where I could express my hurt, my pain, my emotions, my fears and my nightmares.

My mom once told me that God gives everyone a gift. I remember writing a play for my sixth grade class. It was for a PTA meeting at school. It just came to me. The students in the class actually acted it out while I was operating the stage curtains behind the scene. I actually felt comfortable being hidden from view. I would write about the dreams and nightmares that I had in the form of poetry. The words would just flow from within. They were therapeutic for me at the time. It was as if there was this person on the inside of me who was talking to me in a beautiful poetic language. Writing became my friend and at the same time my first love of reading took a back seat because of fear.

Even then, I still wrestled with the nightmares. I was traumatized, but at that age, I didn't know what that meant or how to reach out for help. I never even talked about what I was going through with anyone. It happened so often, I just got used to it.

WAR AMONG THE ANGELS

Thunder, Lightening, Thunder, Lightening.
Bolts of anger shoot across the skies
Roaring shouts from the Man Most High
All of whom are looking down on us
Building up anger and letting their tears fall down.

St. Lucifer, walking amongst the living
Looking for some weak-embedded humans for which he
may tempt
So many, so many are in sight.

Thunder, Lightening
Bolts of anger shoot across the skies
Roaring shouts from the Man Most High
All of whom are looking down on us
Building up anger and letting their tears fall down.

Laughing, laughing, St. Lucifer is laughing
Looking at all the mindless people
Listening to the many lies
Watching the hate grow with every passing second
Watching the earth revolve into ashes
Laughing, laughing, St. Lucifer is laughing.

Thunder, Lightening, **THUNDER, LIGHTENING**
Bolts of anger shoot across the skies
Roaring shouts from the Man Most High
All of whom are looking down on us
Building up anger and letting their tears fall down.

CHAPTER 3

PORTRAIT OF MY MOTHER

My mom was a nurse's aide. She took care of people. She was everything to me. She was the strongest person I knew. I just didn't know how strong she was. In my eyes she could do no wrong. Her job did not allow a lot of time for her to spend with me. I would come home from school and she would be at work. She told me once that she had never completed high school. She would joke with me and tell me she only went to school for one day in her sister's place. I used to believe her but she was so smart.

She would make our clothes in a day. She had one of those antique Singer sewing machines. Sometimes she would use a pattern and sometimes they would be designs of her own. She made pear preserves from the trees in our backyard. She was a great cook. My favorite desserts were her peach cobbler and her chocolate cake. Every Christmas she would bake all of our favorites. She would have a table full of desserts. She would reupholster our furniture, paint the house, mow the lawn, and she had a garden. To me, there was nothing she could not do. Every year or every other year, our house looked remodeled from the inside out and our living room furniture looked brand new when she finished reupholstering it. She was a kind, loving woman; very giving, but she didn't play either.

She was a disciplinarian and did not tolerate nonsense. She kept us in line. She was beautiful both inside and out. Our schools were segregated, so I was not exposed to any other races of people. Our teachers were all black, our community was all black, our schools and our friends were all black. We didn't have access to new books so our school books were used books donated to us from white schools. When we got our first television everything was black and white. That's really the only exposure I can recall with white people, seeing them on TV. My mom was watching TV when they announced that Martin Luther King Jr. was murdered. John F. Kennedy was president and we were having drills at school on what to do in case of bomb threats during the Cuban Missile Crisis.

One day, I went downtown to the post office with my mom. She was mailing her income taxes and the lines were extremely long. There was a white woman in the post office that passed out and fell over on the floor. My mom immediately got out of the line and ran to her aid. I believe the lady was having some sort of episode with her heart. My mom discovered a bottle of pills on the woman and she put one under her tongue. The woman was revived. I had never seen my mom save a life before. I was so in awe and proud of my mother. As badly as we were treated for being black in those days, she saved this woman's life. I believe it was at that moment, I saw people as people, regardless of race or the color of their skin. Life is life and life is valuable and precious. I learned that lesson through my mother's actions that day.

My grandmother had become ill and my mother moved her into our home to take care of her. My sister and I were moved to the front room in the house while our grandmother was in our room. She was closer to our mother's room and it was larger. My grandmother was from Opelousas, Louisiana and her eleven children were raised there. She worked for this white family and was raped by the man she worked for. Black people did not have abortions and she gave birth to a son who looked like he was white. When he was old enough he moved away and cut ties with his family and he passed himself off as a white man. He married a white woman, but they never had children.

Later, my grandmother moved to Washington, Louisiana. When we used to visit her, she didn't have a bathroom so we had to use what was called the outhouse. She had a big, round metal wash tub that we used to bathe in. She would also use it to wash clothes. She would fill it with water and we all had to take a bath in the same water. I was the youngest so the water was cold and dirty when it was my turn. She would keep the tub outside on her back porch to wash her clothes with her scrub board. She had a wood stove she used to cook on. My mother installed wiring in grandma's house herself so that she would have lights. Her bed was so high, you could hardly climb up in it. My grandmother would make the most beautiful quilts. She was an amazing woman, as well.

When she came to live with us, she had this huge lump in the center of her chest. I didn't know it at the time, but she had cancer. I didn't know what was wrong with her but I knew she was very sick. One day my mother was not at home. My grandmother began to call my name. Somehow I was afraid she was going to die, so I hid from her. I was terrified of death from the nightmares that I would have. No one knew about my tormenting dreams because I never talked about them to anyone. I never went to see why she was calling me.

My aunt who lived in Louisiana took my grandmother into her care. It was difficult for my mother to care for her because she had to work. My mother took us to our aunt's house so we could visit with Mom. That's what we called our grandmother. I didn't know that it would be the last time I would see her alive.

One Sunday morning, my mother was standing at the kitchen sink and her sister called her. My mother had been singing gospel songs while cooking and washing dishes. My aunt told her that Mom had just passed away. When my mother hung up the phone, she walked outside, she lifted her arms toward heaven and she thanked God. She stood in the driveway of our house and praised God. I had never seen anyone do that before.

When we went to Mom's funeral, I looked into the casket where she laid and she looked like she was asleep. She was so beautiful and peaceful. I don't ever remember seeing my mother cry. She was all of 5'2", a small woman with a tremendous amount of strength. She was always busy working and taking care of others.

As a little girl, I remember my mother having me kneel at her feet and she would have me repeat the Lord's Prayer. I knew, *"Now I lay me down to sleep. I pray the Lord my soul to keep. If I should die before I wake. I pray the Lord my soul to take."*

We prayed the Lord's Prayer together until I learned to be able to recite it on my own. I knew the words, however, I didn't know its significance because I did not know God. I was reading one of my mother's books and I read Psalm 23. The words were so beautiful to me that I remembered it, not realizing at the time how that Psalm would impact my life forever. To this day I still recite those prayers because they are treasures within my heart. Although I didn't have a relationship with God at the time, I got a glimpse of Him when my mother lifted up her arms when Mom had passed away. I saw another side of my mother that I had not seen before. I can't say I understood it at that time, but truly, one day I would. It wasn't so much the words my mother would speak, but the way she lived that spoke volumes to me.

No doubt, her mom must have passed along her strength to my mother. One day I would understand the lessons of her life and how her strength was passed down to me. She gave me a name at birth which means "strong". I have come to value the significance of the strength these women possessed, the grace they walked in, the way they lived, the way they loved people, and most of all, the way they loved God.

TRIBUTE TO MOM

*I close my eyes to think of her and the many lives she
touched*
*She did not speak a lot of words but her smile would say
so much.*
*Your heart was always lifted when you walked into her
room*
She had no time for sadness
She gave no place to gloom
You never knew the pain she felt
You never saw her fear
*She only showed her faith in God whenever you came
near*
*When you thought she did not understand or that she
was not aware,*
*Her laughter would fill your heart and her smile would
say she cared*
The Lord has called home today
Another precious soul
To go beyond the gates of pearl
To walk on streets of gold
To join the choir of angels
To sing Heaven's song
Her light has gone before us
But her smile lingers on.

CHAPTER 4

PORTRAIT OF MY FATHER

We were a family of eight – my dad, my mom, and six children. My oldest sister was old enough to be my mother. I had three siblings who were much older than me. My oldest sister had a daughter who was only a year younger than I. Her first baby had died.

My earliest memories were that my oldest brother was married and living in a different city, and my next oldest brother was a soldier in Korea. I grew up with my sister and brother who were seven and five years older than I, respectively, so I was alone quite a bit. I was what you would call a "menopausal baby." Technically, according to my parents' biological clocks, I wasn't supposed to be here. My parents were in their forties when I came along.

My dad was a veteran and had served in World War II. I believe that he and my mom were married at the time of his service and he was released early because of health issues. When he was young, he was accidentally shot by a cousin of his. The doctors didn't remove the bullet because of its location. It was a possibility he would die. He lived the rest of his life with that bullet inside of him.

My dad owned his own business. He was a barber and his shop was in the Third Ward. My mom used to work with him as a barber. She told me once that she had to quit because my dad was upset that most of the customers would come to her. She then went to school and became a nurse. He worked Tuesday through Saturday and he was off on Sundays and Mondays. My dad was the head usher at his church. He was also in the choir. When my siblings were growing up, they had no choice but to go to church. I only went to church every now and again. My mom's work schedule prohibited her from attending church regularly, and for that reason, I rarely went. I would spend a lot of time at my oldest sister's house. I practically grew up with her children because of our ages. My mother would pick me up after she got off from work on the weekends.

I used to think my parents were extremely strict. My oldest sister was scary for real. We knew not to cross her because she had no problem beating us. She was a nurse also. When she went to work we would sneak out of the house and go play. If the neighbors saw us doing something we weren't supposed to be doing, we all got a whooping. The neighbors would watch out for us, as well.

I would love to be at home when my dad arrived home from work. He would always bring me candy. M&M's were my favorite. He didn't have anything for my sister and brother, so I think they may have been a little jealous. He was so much harder on them than on me. I was his little girl. On the days he would drive me to school, he would cook breakfast for me and we would eat breakfast together. My dad could sing like an angel. He went to church every Sunday. He was so faithful; at least that's what I thought.

My father had one weakness that I knew of. Every Monday on his off day, he would pull out his whiskey. He mixed it with milk and by the end of the day, he would be sloppy drunk. I was unaware that he used to beat my mother until my older brother was big enough to defend her. Later, I learned that my dad had a weakness for women, as well, and he was unfaithful to our mother. At one point, though, my mother and father were sleeping in separate rooms. I thought it was because of his drinking but it could have been because of the women, as well. My dad would be so intoxicated that he would fall out of bed. I would try to pick him up off the floor. When my mother saw me, she would come to help me. My best friend lived two doors down from us. I was seven days older than her and we were always together. As young teenagers her dad was teaching her how to drive.

One Sunday he took me with them and he let me drive. We were on one of the back streets in our neighborhood and her dad instructed me to back up so I could turn around. We were near a ditch when he instructed me to back up. He told me to stop and to drive forward. I put my foot on the gas and drove into the ditch. I had forgotten to put the gear in forward. I was so afraid. He may have been a bit upset but he didn't get angry with me. The ditch was small and the car wasn't damaged, but it was stuck. A man drove by and helped him pull the car out of the ditch. He wouldn't take any money for helping us. He had just washed his car and he was not pleased that he had to clean it again. That was the end of my driving lessons, though.

One day my dad was drunk and asleep on the couch. We asked him if we could drive his car to the store. He muttered "Um Hum." We then approached her mom and asked her if it was okay for us to go to the corner store and she said yes. We may have neglected to tell her mom that we were going to drive my dad's car. My friend was a much better driver than I was because her dad had been teaching her. She drove to the store and I attempted to drive back home.

Well, on the way home I made a wide turn and almost hit a car. Lo and behold, it was her dad. I almost hit him head on. He told us to take that car back to the house and he would see her back home. She was grounded for two weeks. We were not allowed to see or talk to each other. When I went into the house I told my dad what had happened. I wasn't in trouble because my dad had actually given us permission to take the car. He was still intoxicated and he began to talk to me about my birth. He said that when my mother had told him that she was pregnant, he cursed her. He did not want any more children. He had wanted to give me away to his brother and his wife who was barren. He continued to tell me that my sister had been praying for a baby sister, but when the report came back from the hospital that I was a boy, she was waiting at home with a knife planning to kill me because she didn't want another brother. My dad did not look at me for two weeks after my mother brought me home. He continued to tell me what a good daughter I was; how I would always attempt to help him up from the floor when he had fallen down. Even though he didn't want another child back then, I was his favorite. Out of all the things he shared with me that day about how much he loved me and how proud he was of me, all I could hear was "I didn't want you. I cursed the day when you were conceived."

When I graduated from high school, my dad left us. It was just me and my mother at home then. They were divorced and he went on with his life and my mother was left alone. He had property in Third Ward. His barber shop was in front, facing the main street, and behind his shop he had a one bedroom house. I was attending college at the time.

I went to church with him one day. On the way, he stopped to pick up his lady friend. He wanted me to get in the back seat and I was so angry with him I didn't move. She was much younger than he was. The crazy thing is she looked like a younger version of my mom. He had thoughts of marrying her but he never did. She had an aneurysm and she passed away. He actually told me about his cheating on my mother. He shared that with me after my mother had passed and he was up in age. He just loved being with women. He also told me that my mother was the only woman he truly ever loved. Actually, the day he divorced her, when they walked out of the courtroom he told her he had made a mistake, but she would not take him back.

Years later when I was pregnant with my fourth child and my mother had been diagnosed with Alzheimer's, my brother convinced them to remarry. And they did. He wasn't able to take care of her by himself but I do believe that she was the only woman he ever truly loved. God knows how to turn things around when life turns upside down.

THOUGHTS

Looking out, looking far beyond distant horizons
Searching, longing, seeking a new life
Thinking, far beyond man's imagination
Wanting to be a part of something real but yet untouched
Walking alone on one of life's empty highways
Traveling on in search for yourself
Existing in a time of premeasured fantasies
Loving the life, but not living
Being a part of youth, happiness, and everlasting peace
Being a part of solitude and thoughts
Drifting away on a distant dream
Thinking you were a star shining over the world
Being the universe within yourself
A new life within your reach, but yet so distant and unreal
Life, a mere way of saying, you belong
Hoping you will always belong to your thoughts.

CHAPTER 5

ON MY OWN, ALL ALONE

I had graduated in the top ten percent of my class. My counselor talked to my mother about a summer program at Prairie View A&M University where I could attend the program for free. My mother didn't make enough money for me to go to college, but she made too much for me to qualify for grant money.

My mother drove me to the college to enroll me in the summer program. While we were waiting in the lobby of the administration building to get me enrolled in the school program, this gentleman in a suit approached us. He greeted us with a smile and began to ask questions. He inquired about my interest of study, and I told him I wanted to study law. He asked me about my high school grades and when I told him that I had graduated in the top ten percent of my class, he asked me if I would be interested in the engineering program. Engineering was also a part of the summer program they were offering. He said he was the assistant dean of engineering and he indicated that I could possibly be eligible for a scholarship. I had never even heard the word engineering, let alone know what it meant, but I was not about to turn down a free education. He instructed me to come by the engineering building on the following morning to meet there with the dean of engineering. My mother made sure I got enrolled in the summer program and settled into the dormitory.

As I watched her drive off, heading back home to Houston, I cried. I had never been on my own before. I was happy to see some of my high school friends there in the dorm. I didn't feel so alone. Later on that day, while I was with my high school friends, there was a group of young boys who were part of the Omega Psi Phi fraternity fooling around at our dormitory. They were trying to either impress us or intimidate us. I was neither. When I was in elementary school, we would fight on purpose, so I was not afraid to defend myself. One of these boys was trying to impress me and I let him know right then that I was not the one to be messed with. Even though I didn't know God, He certainly was working in my life. That young man is presently my husband of 44 years.

I met with the dean of engineering the following day and he offered me a full scholarship in engineering as long as I kept a minimum 3.0 grade average. The assistant dean changed the course of my life. I know now that it was God orchestrating my life. I met this young man who was majoring in mechanical engineering, and we started dating. He was a year older than I was, and we shared the same birthday. He appeared to be really nice and smart, and since we shared the same birthday, I thought we had a lot in common. We got along really well. He had an undesirable issue, however.

One evening, he was walking me to my dormitory. For no uncertain reason he slapped me. I snapped and started fighting back. Apparently he wanted to control and manipulate me. I was so angry and hurt. He discovered really early that I had a temper and I wasn't afraid to fight. I had gone on dates when I was in high school, but I had never been in a close, long term relationship with anybody. I was still a virgin. I didn't mess around like that. He was the first boy I was intimate with. Others had tried, but I wasn't ready for that. Also, I was afraid of my mother. Maybe I was infatuated with him because we shared the same birthday and I assumed we had a lot in common. I actually thought I was in love with him. He was kind, caring, smart, a bit goofy and fun to be with until he wasn't. We would often study together, as well. I was majoring in electrical engineering. We didn't have any classes together, but he was a good tutor. It was as if he had a dual personality because he had no problem fighting me. I guess I really didn't know him at all. I had no problem defending myself either.

One day we were in the cafeteria for lunch. I saw him with another girl and when I walked up to his table, he basically blew me off. I was so angry as I walked away that as I passed this student's table, I picked up his drink, walked over to my boyfriend's lunch table, and threw the drink in his face. Then I turned and walked away. I had a sneaky suspicion that he would retaliate, so I grabbed the knife from my tray and took it with me. I was right. He was waiting for me by a building I had to walk by to get to my dormitory. I was ready.

When I saw him I told him about my brothers and that I knew where he lived. With my knife, which was dull by the way, in my hand, I told him if he touched me that my brothers would be under the jail after they finished with him. Somehow that threat worked because he didn't hit me that day, and he knew I was serious. We were still together, but he never attempted to fight me again.

I went to school year round. I really enjoyed college. In my third year of college, though, I recall this one day where I had slipped into a deep depression. I took a whole bottle of pills and laid down to sleep. I had made the decision that I didn't want to live anymore. I had fallen into a deep sleep when I heard a knock at the door. It woke me up. I opened the door and there was this girl at the door looking for someone named Valerie. Well, that's my name, but I had never seen her before, nor did I ever see her again. She apologized for disturbing me and she left. I was startled, but looking back to that day, I often wondered if she was an angel sent by God to rescue me. After she left, I went to the student center to get something to eat because I felt really sick. I ran into a friend and we just talked. There were periods in my life where depression and sadness would hit me. I had moments when I didn't want to live. It may have been because of the nightmares and the things I went through as a child, or the rejection I felt from my father. I never talked to anyone about the way I felt, but I never attempted to take my life again. I would just cry myself to sleep. I really didn't think anyone noticed or if anyone cared.

I still dated the young man from time to time. We would make up and break up. He took me home with him one weekend to meet his mom and siblings. When he pulled up to his house, I had a deja-vu moment immediately. I had seen this before. I had a dream while I was in high school where I saw this house. It was quite similar to the house I lived in. Before he ever took me into his house, I already knew where the rooms were. It was built on the same floor plan as the house I lived in. What is going on? I was dating a man who shared my birthday and now the place where he grew up in another city looks like the house I was raised in? What did all of this mean?

I graduated from high school in 1974 in the top 10 percent of my class when I was 17 years old. I graduated with honors from PVAMU in the winter of 1977 – a semester early. I made it. During my time at Prairie View, I was the only female who had graduated as an electrical engineer. There were other female engineering students there, but they majored in mechanical engineering. I finished six months early with honors. I was so happy. I had friends. I had pledged a sorority, so I had sisters. In that same month, I was dating my future husband. I had landed a job in the space industry and my life was great. Things were happening so fast and I was so excited about how my life was turning out. Up until then, I was living my best life until...my sister and I decided to go to a nightclub and I was right back living a nightmare. BUT...**I heard His voice.**

I SEARCHED FOR YOU IN THE DARKNESS

I searched for You in the darkness
I was hungry, I was thirsty, I was lost, but You were nowhere to be found
I needed to know You were real so I asked others who I thought knew You
They did not give me the answer I was seeking
There was no one to tell me how to find You
You were drawing me, but I could not see You
You were calling me, yet I could not hear You
I was walking through the darkness and I felt so all alone
But, You were there in the darkest hour of my life
You heard the cries of my heart which no one else could hear
As I prepared myself for death
You came to rescue me
And I heard your voice piercing through the darkness
You will not die
Through the void, I knew You were there
And I was at peace, and I knew that I was not alone
You waited patiently for me to surrender my heart and life to You
You brought me out of the darkness into Your Marvelous Light
And I would be transformed forever.

CHAPTER 6

FACING MY DEMONS

My sister took me to the police station the following day. I surrendered my clothing and undergarments to the police, as I'm sure they became part of the evidence. I was then placed in a room with a book of possible criminals. After looking through this book, I picked out two men whom I thought looked like them. I wasn't sure it was them. I doubted and I questioned myself because I was so afraid.

My sister was strong, though. I didn't think she was afraid of anything. She worked in a building behind the police department where they sold guns and supplied the police force, so she knew quite a few of the officers. I can't be certain, but because they knew her, they would leave no stone unturned to find these guys.

My oldest brother had come from out of town and showed up at my mother's house. He, my youngest brother and my future husband took me for a ride. It was nighttime and it was dark. They wanted me to show them the place where they raped me. I wasn't good with directions because I didn't venture out on my own very much. I still don't. But with the information I had stored in my mind and had put on paper, they drove me to the location. My two brothers exited the car and went to look for the apartment. They were going to confront these men. I was so afraid. They came back to the car without finding them and we went home.

It wasn't until years later when I learned they were armed and had every intention of taking care of these men themselves. My younger brother had served in the Vietnam War. I'm glad they did not find them. I would have been sick if they had gotten into trouble.

Again, I saw God's hand at work. I had to go to the police station to view a lineup, and I was able to point the two men out. I still had my doubts, but it was them.

My fiancé and I were married within the next two months of the rape. His dad was the kindest man I had ever met. His mom and I didn't really hit it off at first. When I met her, I had been raped and I was pregnant. We hadn't dated long, so I'm sure I wasn't the model person she would want for her son. She really didn't know very much about me. She really didn't think I was good enough for her son, and she was not yet convinced that our unborn child was his. What I didn't realize then was that rejection had followed me throughout my life. Sadness and depression were rejection's companions.

We lived with my mom initially because I felt safe there. We both had jobs and my mom was a nurse. She and my husband got along really well, and it actually worked out for us. They both took really good care of me during this time. My husband would drink a lot. He was a party man, but he was hurting, as well, and going through his own trauma over what had happened to me, to us.

Seven months after the rape we had to go to court where I saw those men for the first time in months. I was petrified. The trial was reset for a different date. I was so glad to get out of there. I was eight to eight and a half months pregnant when the trial began. The men chose a trial by judge with no jury. I suppose I was meant to be intimidated by having a closed trial. There was no jury and my family could not be in the room with me. One of my husband's fraternity brothers was there to witness the trial. Instead of being afraid and intimidated, my hormones must have kicked in because I was just angry.

My sister, my brother and his friend were the only three people with me. The two rapists were in the room with me. However, when they were being questioned, my husband's friend was the only one allowed in the courtroom as a spectator. My parents were not there because I didn't want them there. I didn't want them to go through that, but I was glad I was not alone. When it was time for the verdict, the judge's ruling was "*Guilty.*"

I was called into a private room with the court appointed lawyer who had represented me, and he asked me questions that would determine their sentencing. To this day, they have become a vague memory. I don't remember their names. I don't recall what they look like. They would have to appear in court a few weeks after for the sentencing, which was held on September 11, 1978. I don't remember them at all, but I remember the date. Although, I was not able to attend.

My baby boy was born on that day. He was beautiful. He was a healthy 7 lb 10 1/2 oz baby boy. He was my special gift from God. I went into labor on Sunday and he was born at 1:06 am Monday morning. The irony of it all. The rape ended early Sunday morning, and that same Sunday, I discovered I had a life growing inside of me who would keep me sane, give me hope, save my life, bring me joy and teach me to love. The day those two men were sentenced was the same day my beautiful baby was born. When something ended, something new began in my life.

My husband and I had been attending church pretty regularly. He grew up in church, but I didn't. I was out of touch with religion, but I enjoyed our visits to church. We left the big church that my in-laws attended to join a small church closer to home. My husband and I were in our apartment by then. My sister lived close to the pastor's family, which was also close to the neighborhood I grew up in. The church actually started in the pastor's home and graduated to a funeral home. He had access to the building and we had choir rehearsals and church services there. Eventually, we were able to move into a small building where we had church services.

After some time, my husband and I were able to buy our own home. We moved in shortly before our second child was born. Our children were our delight. We have four children - two boys and two girls. They were born three years apart, and all four of them were born on a Monday. Our fourth child had not been born yet when my mother began exhibiting signs of Alzheimer's. I actually tricked her into coming to live with us. I made her think it was her idea.

While she was with us, she would help me with the kids but it was evident that she was getting worse. While she was with us, I had decided to go to a community college to take music classes. I had started writing again and I wanted to put my poetry to music. I was only there one semester because my husband had an issue with me not being home with the kids and my mother.

We were actually members of that church for several years. I was able to take my mother to church, as well. My elder brother had convinced my mom and dad to remarry. I believe she went along with it because she wanted to go back home. She had forgotten why they divorced in the first place. She did not like the turmoil that was going on in our house. I was actually pregnant with our fourth child on the day my parents remarried.

My mother's condition began to worsen, so my eldest sister, who was a nurse, took her into her home to look after her. Through the years, my husband stopped attending church. My kids and I continued to go to church. I knew God was real but I thought He was far away in the heavens. I was still having issues in my life. I had experienced a lot of healing, yet God was not through with me. I had never been taught that I needed to be delivered.

One day I was so angry with God and I told Him that if He was who He said He was and I was supposed to belong to Him, then there should be something different about my life. I was still a sinner and I knew it. I was still broken, angry, and mean to a degree. I shouted those words out to God and I quit going to church.

There was a church close to our home and the pastor lived down the street from us. He asked if they could take our kids to church and I said yes. He and his wife were very kind and caring people. My kids loved going to church and the van would stop by our house to pick them up for service and drop them back off at home. My husband seemed to be more interested in partying with his friends, going to clubs and drinking. We were drifting further and further apart. I started going out, as well, with coworkers from my job.

One of my work friends noticed my life was spiraling out of control and she invited me to her house. She had been talking to me about her experience with being filled with the Holy Spirit. The night before I went to her house, I decided to quit drinking and smoking cigarettes. I saved my last cigarette and just before midnight I smoked it and went to sleep. When I arrived at her house she talked and I listened. Then she began to pray. The only person I ever recalled praying for me was my mother; another irony.

My friend and I also shared the same birthday. She was one year older than me. She and my boyfriend in college were born on the same day. As she was praying for me, I was weeping almost uncontrollably. When she stopped praying I felt such peace like I never felt before.

We went to her back porch and stood outside. As I was standing there, I looked toward the fence in her backyard and I could see a white figure standing near the rear fence. I saw the image and I was intently trying to figure out what I was seeing. She began to scream with excitement, *"I see the Holy Ghost all over you!"* She had startled me, so I took my eyes off of Him and when I looked again, He was gone. When I went to work the next day, I noticed that the smell of smoke made me sick. I had no desire to even be around smoke. I was totally set free. It was at that moment that I knew that God could deliver and set me free from anything that would try to keep me in bondage.

My family was always close. We didn't all live in close proximity but we took care of each other. When my brother was home for good from Vietnam, he was not in a good place. He married his first wife when he was 18 – right before he went to serve his country. When his tour of duty was complete, he had changed. He was not the boy he used to be when he left home to fight in that war. He came home and he brought some baggage with him.

He was paranoid. He was also addicted to drugs, both resulting from his experiences during the Vietnam War. For years, he suffered from PTSD and drug addiction. He and my husband did not get along well. They had a strong dislike for one another. I could not abandon my family. My family had always been by side and was always there to protect me. My relationship with my family caused even more problems.

In 1986, our company lost a major contract with NASA. Many of the employees were going to work for the company who won the contract. I had the opportunity to go to work in the Washington DC area. I had even petitioned for my husband to get a job with the same people, however, he did not want to relocate. At the time, I was pregnant with child number four, and the other company would not hire me because of it. I was able to take FMLA with my current employer so I did receive a portion of my salary. After the baby was born, and it was time for me to go back to work, I was terminated. By this time we were bombarded with bills and deeply in debt.

We actually ended up filing bankruptcy. There was a period in my life that my marriage was so bad that everything was spiraling out of control. I went to work for Chevron gas station down the street from our house. It was convenient for me because I was close to my children and could be home in minutes. It was so embarrassing for me and I was ashamed of myself. I had an engineering degree. I worked as an engineer for ten years. Here I find myself with four kids, in debt beyond measure, in a failing marriage, and working at a gas station. I applied for a job with Continental Airlines and got the job.

However, everything else was out of control. I was at one of the lowest points of my life. I would hate for my husband to come home. I had gotten to the point that I didn't care if he stayed out with his friends. I had enough and decided that I could no longer live like this. I felt like the burden and responsibility was strictly on my shoulders. The manager at the gas station was also hired with Continental. We had become good friends so she said I could move in with her. I packed up my kids and left.

She had a two bedroom apartment, so my four kids and I were all cramped up in one room, sleeping in one bed. She would wake up early in the morning and read her Bible and pray. I didn't do either. I took care of my kids, drove them to and from school, and worked. I knew that she was growing tired of us because we had invaded her space and my kids were a bit lively. When they broke a window to her front door, I knew that it was an indication for me to go.

I was having a really difficult time. I had met this woman whose son was in the rehab center with my brother. She was very sweet, kind and we became really close friends. I went to visit her one day at her home. She lived alone but took care of her grandson who had special needs. I could tell that her life had been a struggle, yet she did not complain. My children and I would visit my brother at the rehab center on weekends. The kids enjoyed the visits because of the treats.

This wonderful lady would become a voice of reason in my life. She told me how she raised her kids alone. Being out in the world alone with my kids and not really having a place of my own taught me some valuable lessons. I began to ponder how difficult it would be for me to raise my kids on my own. At that particular time, I had no place to call my own, no money and no help. I had asked my husband for $2.00 one day to buy the kids something to eat and he told me no.

One night while he was on his way home, he fell asleep and drove his new white truck into the garage of a minister's house. He totaled his truck and caused a lot of damage to the man's house. The insurance covered the cost. The interesting thing is that the preacher came to the house and invited my husband to church. The church was only a five minute drive and I had passed by it almost daily taking the kids to school for years. The school was too far to walk and too close to ride the bus. I would often wonder about that church. My mom was sick at the time. I would cry out to God because I could not talk to my mother to ask for her counsel and guidance. I wanted my mother. I didn't realize it at the time but God had orchestrated this woman into my life. She would take me under her wings. She was a spiritual mother to me. Here again, it was a divine setup by God. She invited me to her church – Lakewood.

It was a Spirit-filled church. I was afraid of it because I had not been exposed to people speaking and praying in an unknown tongue. I didn't go back right away. After spending time with her, though, my heart began to change. I began to humble myself. I decided to go back home to try to make my marriage work. I did not want my kids growing up without their father. Being out there on my own was more difficult than I had imagined.

When we came back home, my life began to change. I began to help my sister take care of my mom. When I went back home, I started dreaming again. They were not nightmares. The dreams would change the course of my life. One night I dreamed of the Lord coming down from the sky as a baby in His mother's arms. The closer He drew near, He appeared as a full grown man. I saw Him walking in the air where He was hand picking people out of those who were standing there watching Him. When He reached me, He would look at me and pass me up. I was disturbed by this dream and I knew that I needed to change my life. I thought He had rejected me. I would pray and ask Him to forgive me of all of my sins. But, I would have this dream more than once.

I began going back to visit Lakewood. I was nervous and a bit afraid because the people would be speaking in a language I did not understand. I was drawn back because of this beautiful woman God had placed in my life. I didn't realize that she was on assignment to bring me closer to God and to bring healing in my life. While I was there, I witnessed people being filled with the Holy Ghost. The altars would be full of people coming forth for salvation. People were getting healed and delivered. It was different from anything I had experienced and I started attending quite often.

My spiritual mom had a daughter. You would never guess, but we had the same birthday. She invited me to go to AZUSA with her in Oklahoma. All of my clothes were black. I didn't realize that I surrounded myself with darkness and depression. My spiritual mom made me a dress and gave me some spending money. Because I was employed by Continental Airlines, we were able to fly for a tremendously reduced rate. We arrived in Tulsa, Oklahoma and this trip transformed my life.

There was an altar call given by Joyce Meyers for those who wanted to be filled with the Holy Spirit. I was sitting in the top of the rafters at the Coliseum and I began to hear the word "*Glory*" over and over again. It was as if I was being called and drawn to make my way down to the altar. The altar workers were giving me instructions on how to receive the baptism of the Holy Spirit. They told me that I didn't have to beg for it. I really didn't understand. People around me began to speak in an unknown tongue, but I didn't know how to receive Him. It didn't work for me. I was practically begging God but nothing happened.

I left the altar disappointed, but I had so much peace. When we got back to the room I talked for hours and told my friend everything about my life – the good, the bad, and the ugly. I confessed my sins. While I was confessing to her, she was praying in her spiritual language beneath her breath. It was well into the evening when I stopped talking. I was so hungry for God that when I took a bath, I sank myself in the tub beneath the water, asking the Lord to cleanse me and to baptize me. When I woke up the next morning, everything was so bright. Colors were bright. I was tremendously joyful and full of peace. I couldn't wait to wear my new dress that my spiritual mom made for me.

There was an interruption in the service that had been announced for women only. The minister's name was T. D. Jakes. His sermon was *"Woman, Thou Art Loosed."* I had never experienced anything like it. He talked about the woman who was bowed over for eighteen years. Jesus interrupted his teaching and turned to this woman and said *"Woman, Thou Art Loosed"* and immediately this woman was set free. The building erupted with this message. As I sat there listening to his words, I felt that God was speaking directly to me. When he instructed us to lift up our hands to God and worship, He spoke those words again: *"Woman, Thou Art Loosed."* I fell to the floor in the rafters, but it felt like I was laid down. I wasn't hurt. I felt no pain.

When I got up off of the floor, I felt washed, cleansed from the inside out. I saw Jesus as a shadow on the cross. As He spoke to me, I could hear, and my eyes were open where I could see Him. The color became so bright and light was illuminating. For the first time in my life, I felt truly free. He set me free. I felt so light and so full of joy. The building was filled with worship, prayer and the presence of God.

Bishop Jakes instructed us to sow an eighteen dollar seed, which represented the eighteen years that this woman was in bondage. I was so excited that I took out my checkbook and wrote an eighteen dollar check to AZUSA. I didn't even have eighteen dollars in my bank account, but I sowed it in faith. I wanted all of God. Everything was so bright.

When we were on the way back home and seated on the plane ready to take off, I opened my Bible to Genesis 1:1. The words were alive. In the beginning, God. What I heard in my spirit was God, God, GOD. It was God the Father, God the Son, and God the Holy Spirit. At that point, I asked Him within my heart, "*God, where did You come from?*" I heard Him say, "*GOD.*" In Him there is no beginning and there is no end because He is Infinite.

When I arrived home, I was not the same. When I opened my mouth to speak, it was Revelations that proceeded out of me. It felt like fire was on my body, but it didn't burn. I think my husband was afraid of me. He must have thought something was wrong with me, but he recognized that something was different.

I could not sleep. I laid in bed all night and throughout the next day, reading the Bible and listening to the Spirit of God. There was so much revelation I was getting from the Word of God. I could not get past the first chapter of Genesis. I could hear the words. They were alive.

On the following day, I was still in the first chapter of Genesis. Then, I heard the voice of God say, "*Give me your son.*" I had two sons, but I didn't know which one He was talking about. My response to God was "*You can have all four of my children.*" I never asked Him which son He wanted because I gave Him all of them - my sons and my daughters.

A few days later, the eighteen dollar check was sent to my home from the AZUSA Conference, uncashed with "*insufficient funds.*" I sent the eighteen dollars back. I had never experienced anything so beautiful and wonderful in my life. There was a reverence in my home and so much joy filled the atmosphere. The next time I went to Lakewood, I responded to the call for baptism. My daughters wanted to be baptized, as well. When we went back to the evening service with our change of clothes the three of us were baptized together.

IN THE GARDEN

Walking in the garden in the cool of the day
Seeking solitude and refuge and a solemn place to pray
Treacherous storms are raging, trouble on every hand
Wrestling over matters I can not understand
Tired, alone, and weary with trials I must endure
I enter that place of rest in Him and lift up praises to my
Lord
He meets me by the stream where the waters are crystal
clear
But while I'm in His Presence, all my burdens disappear
He settles my troubled soul and dries up all my tears
He fills me with His love as He takes my hand in His
He gives me gifts of peace and joy to carry on my way
We'll meet again tomorrow in the cool of the day
...In the garden.

CHAPTER 7

HUNGRY

I was so hungry to know more. We lived about a five minute drive from Gulf Meadows Church. I had passed by this church so many times. When I drove by the church I always seemed to be curious about it, but I never would go in.

While I was at AZUSA, I had run into a friend that I worked with when I was at the Space Center. She informed me of a Prayer Meeting at Gulf Meadows every Tuesday morning and told me to check it out. I wanted more of God, so one morning I went.

It was a Spirit-filled church like Lakewood. The Spirit of God was there. This church had prayer 7 days a week. Services were held on Wednesday night and Sundays at 8am, 11am, and 7pm. I was so hungry and thirsty for God that I was there every time the doors opened. There was a Spanish Prayer Meeting on Sunday evening before the service that I attended, and I didn't even know the language. However, I recognized His presence. I would walk into the sanctuary on Sunday morning and lift up my heart to God in worship. I would just bask in His presence. People thought I was snobbish because I wouldn't speak to them. I just wasn't aware of them because I was totally focused on God.

My beautician at that time was Spirit-filled and she would have books out on a table in her shop. She would allow me to bring some home to read them. I went to church so much that my husband would be upset with me. We actually had a fight one night because he took my keys to prevent me from going to church. I received so much healing and deliverance in my life during this season. I had fallen in love with Jesus and it was no turning back for me. I loved God and these people I went to church with. The worship was glorious. The pastor truly walked in God's presence.

I remember one evening, he had all of us remove our shoes because he said the ground was holy. He didn't preach that evening. We worshiped God. It was an amazing season in my life. My children would be there with me. This church had so much to offer us. The kids had the chance to go to camp. They grew there too. If I would leave the house going to work and did not have my Bible with me, I would turn around and go back to get it.

It was evident that I was not the same person. My eldest sister and my husband would talk about me. She thought I had lost my mind and suggested that my husband should get me some help. My sister was a nurse and she thought I should be committed to a mental institution. I had lost my mind, my heart, my life for I had totally fallen in love with God. He restored my love for poetry and writing. I could not get enough. The poems were different, though, because they would come from within me as a song.

I mentioned earlier that I had gone to school to take a music class. The songs were within me, but I knew nothing about music, how to write it or how to play a musical instrument. I remember when I was young my parents asked me if I wanted to play an instrument and I told them I wanted to play the piano. A piano was outside of what they could afford. They asked me for another choice and I said "the drums." That wasn't going to work because that would be too noisy. I had given up on that dream.

When the songs began to flow from within me, I enrolled in college so that I could learn to put them to music. I really enjoyed the class, but could only take the course one semester. Being a wife, a mother, and helping with the care of my mother took precedence over my interest in music. I would be on my knees talking and praying to God and I would begin to sing to Him. Sometimes I would fall asleep on my knees while praying. I was like a sponge. I wanted to know Him more.

While my sister was caring for our mother, she became a bit overwhelmed. Her eldest daughter was in nursing school and her youngest daughter was working. They lived together along with my mother, and there were three children in the house, as well. We were able to get some assistance for our mother, so we paid someone to help with her care while my sister was working. Her daughters and I would help with my mother when we could. She was walking then, and occasionally she would unlock the door and leave the house.

One day my niece found her in a Sears store with a basket full of clothes. She was walking out of the store, so my niece pushed the cart back inside the store and took her home. My sister admitted her to a nursing home for her safety. She had pretty much quit talking. She had been in about three different homes. When I came back from AZUSA, I quit my job and I brought my mother to our house. She was bedridden by then, and she had a feeding tube. I wasn't a nurse, but I prayed and asked God to help me take care of my mother. My sister would come by to visit and make sure I was doing everything right. She would treat her like a patient, but I was her daughter and God equipped me with everything I needed. She was my mother so I couldn't treat her like a patient.

My sister would come to the house and tie her to the bed. Mother would often pull her tube out and I would have to rush her to the emergency room. I understood that my sister followed the protocols of what they did in the hospital but I could not bring myself to tie her hands to the bed.

The worse she got, the harder it was for me to see her in that condition, but I would do it all over again if I had the chance. My husband would watch her for me whenever I went to church. Somehow, it just worked out and I believe it drew my husband and I closer. We still had some of the same issues, but it didn't bother me like it did in the past. He thought I went over the edge with religion, but that wasn't it. I had a relationship with the Father, the Son, and the Holy Spirit. I was learning, and God was healing me in the process. I was growing in the spirit. Everything was so new and refreshing to me. There was so much joy surrounding me. I literally would absorb books. Anything and everything I could learn about God, I wanted to know. I would go to sleep at night with books in my bed and the Bible under my pillow. I absolutely loved praise and worship.

I began to listen to praise and worship music all of the time. I was playing gospel and my husband was playing R&B. We were as different as night and day. God was my first thought in the morning and my last thought at night. I would talk to Him all during the day. Every chance I had, I was reading the word of God. He truly was first and foremost in my life. I had scriptures posted on my mother's bedroom wall. I would play gospel music for her, as well. I was addicted to Jesus. He truly was and is my very best friend. I was His and He was mine.

I HUNGER FOR YOUR PRESENCE

God, I am in awe of You
I begin to weep at the mention of Your name
You are more precious to me
Than anything or anyone I've ever known
Words can not express the way I feel
Nor can pictures capture the glory of Your splendor
My heart is full and I am overwhelmed
Yet my soul yearns for more of You
The more I know of You, the more I realize
That I don't really know You
There is no limit to You God
And yet, I search for the height of You
I long for the depth of You
My heart cries out to know the breadth of You
I hunger for Your Presence.

CHAPTER 8

THE FATHER'S HEART

I thought I was in a good place. I was rooted and grounded in a church where I was growing in God, loving people, learning to serve and truly loving God. I would check in on my dad from time to time. To be honest, I loved him, but I didn't really respect him. I knew he used to abuse my mother, although I never witnessed it. He was an alcoholic when I was growing up. He had to quit drinking when he was told he was diabetic and had to be on insulin. He really started taking better care of himself. He went to church every Sunday my whole life, and in his 80's he was still chasing women.

I popped up at the house one day to check in on him and he wouldn't let me in. He was not alone. His visits to my mother were rare, but he knew she was in good hands. I recall one Thanksgiving Eve, a church friend and I spent the day baking cookies to give to the homeless. My husband and I had been in debt for years. I had 22 credit cards alone. I understood what it meant to rob Peter to pay Paul. It was evident I still had some unresolved issues in my life. We had no food for Thanksgiving. I called my dad and asked him to loan me $50.00 so I could have Thanksgiving dinner for my kids. He said, "No." I was so hurt that my dad said no that I began to feel rejected by him all over again.

On Thanksgiving morning, my ex-sister-in-law arrived at my house with a smoked ham. She said that she and her husband had been barbecuing and she thought about me. After she left, a friend of mine who lived way across town appeared at my house. She brought so much food over, already cooked, and said

---

she thought about me. She had so much food at home that she wanted to share it with me. You must know, I was crying like a baby.

I was so humbled because what my own dad would not do for me, I knew that my Heavenly Father did it. I believe He was showing me and teaching me that He would supply all of my needs, and that He loved me unconditionally. God did it just for me. I learned that even when I didn't ask Him, my tears were liquid prayers. God answers the sincere cries of one's heart.

My mom had taken her feeding tube out and I had to take her to the hospital. For some reason, her doctor would not come to see her. She had a small heart attack that I was not aware of and they sent her home. I knew she was ill. I prayed and asked God to honor her will and His will for her life.

The next morning, the hospital called and told me to bring her back to the hospital because the cardiologist had seen the heart attack on the monitor. I was so angry I didn't want to take her back there, but they told me they would not be held responsible if anything happened. It would be on me because they called and informed me that she was in danger of dying. So, I took her back to the hospital and they admitted her immediately. She was placed in the ICU.

The following morning I was alone in my mother's bedroom weeping and talking to God. I was really afraid that she was going to die. I heard God tell me, "I love you." My response to Him was, "I don't really know what that is because my own dad doesn't love me." There was a book that my husband had gotten from his mother called "Jesus Loves Me," and God led me to read this book. I took the book to the hospital with me. I never got beyond the first chapter. I cried.

Even though I had told God to honor her will, I pleaded with Him that I wasn't ready.

My dad never visited her while she was in the ICU. It wasn't until later that I discovered he was afraid of hospitals. Only one person could visit her at a time, so me and my sister would take turns. My sister and I would be there practically all day in the ICU waiting room. She was motionless and she was sedated. There were other people in the ICU waiting room as well. One guy was dying of AIDS, and his friends and family were there. All the while, we were there, I was speaking to them about the love of God, and we were sharing our stories. We were all going through this together. There was a chapel in the hospital and I recall praying with a woman in the chapel whose loved one was in the ICU as well.

I would pray for their loved ones when I went home. Somehow, I felt like the guy with AIDS wasn't going to make it. I began to wonder whether or not he had a relationship with God. When I returned to the hospital alone on the following day, his friends were all surrounding his bed. As I passed by the room, I asked them if it was okay for me to pray for him. They gave me permission to pray with him, but they said that he was heavily sedated. He would probably not hear me. I closed my eyes and began to pray. I had never done that before – praying for someone who was dying. I felt the presence of God in that room while I was praying. I opened my eyes and while I was still praying, he was looking at me. His eyes were wide open and he was looking directly at me. I began to talk to him, telling him how Jesus loved him. His parents walked in the room, and part of me felt like I was intruding. They were very cordial, but I knew they were saddened that their son was about to die. When I went home, his parents were on my heart. As I was praying for all of them, the words of a poem began to flow from within me.

I went to visit my mother the next day and she had been moved to a private room. She was no longer in the ICU. She was alert. I had hoped to see the young man's parents at the hospital so I could give them the poem I had written for them, but I didn't go to the ICU that day. God had answered my prayer and brought my mother back to me.

When I was leaving the hospital, his mom and dad were walking out at the same time. They told me that he had just passed away. They thanked me for praying for their son. They shared that they had wanted to find a priest to come and pray for him, but they didn't find one. They were so grateful and appreciative that I prayed with him. We talked for a bit and I handed them the poem I had written for them the night before. They thanked me and hugged me as we said our goodbyes.

I didn't think to pray the prayer of salvation when the young man had opened his eyes. I was upset with myself and wept throughout the day because I thought I had disappointed God. I did know that the Lord was in the ICU while I was praying. I have to believe that what I didn't say, the Lord was speaking to this man. In his darkest hour, I must believe he heard the same voice that I heard so many years ago.

The thief who was on the cross only asked Jesus to remember him when He returns to his kingdom. He didn't ask for forgiveness. He just asked Him to remember him. Jesus' response was, "Today you will be with me in Paradise." What a mighty God we serve. My mother was the only person in the ICU who was released from the hospital. God gave me more time with her. She was assigned a visiting nurse who would come to our home to care for her three times a week. She would bathe her, make her bed, check her vital signs, and always was very pleasant. Not only did God keep her alive, He answered my prayer, sent us help, and showed me that He loved me as a Father would love His daughter.

ON MY WAY HOME

How sweet it is to take this walk
Along God's peaceful shore
To cross the great horizon
And ascend to heaven's door.

Oh, the joy to see my Savior's face
As He waits near His throne
To feel His touch, to hear His voice
As He welcomes me home.

No more pain, no more sorrow
No more tears, I'll ever shed
Forever in God's Presence
Reaping boundless joy instead.

I must say goodbye now
I'll look for you someday
God needs me now in Heaven
To help others find their way.

We will meet again someday
Along God's peaceful shore
Remember that I love you all
But God loves you more.

Dedicated to the parents of the young man in ICU

CHAPTER 9

PREPARATION

God had given me a year with my mother before He called her home. When I had brought her to our house I was honored to be able to take care of her. Her sisters came from out of town to visit her. I didn't get it at the time, but people were coming to visit her to say good-bye. She was beginning to show signs of weakness and I was taking her to the hospital more often.

One night in church, the pastor gave me word that she was getting ready to cross the Jordan. I had an older cousin who was Spirit-filled whom God had recently connected to my life. She came by the house after church one Sunday. She prayed for my mother. She told me my mother's lungs were filling with fluid and it was time to let her go. I didn't know how to let her go. I was so afraid that I would find her gone when I woke that I would sleep on the floor next to her hospital bed.

One day that week, I had to call the ambulance to come and take her to the hospital. She had pneumonia. They took her to a different hospital, which was closer to our house. This time she had no access to her regular doctors. My sister had decided that she wanted her back so she could take care of her. She began making arrangements so that when they released our mother she would be coming home with her. I began to cry out to God to take her home. I didn't think anyone, including my sister, would love her and care for her as I did. I was so grieved that I would no longer be able to take care of her. My cousin and I were at the hospital for a visit with her and my cousin instructed me to read John 14:1-4 to her. So I began to read those scriptures: "*Let not your heart be troubled: ye believe in God, believe also in me.*

In my Father's house are many mansions: if it were not so, I would have told you. I go and prepare a place for you. I will come again, and receive you unto myself: that where I am, there you may be also. And whither I go ye know, and the way ye know."

I then asked my mother if she was ready to go home to be with God and she nodded yes. As my sister was making preparations to take her to her home, the hospital staff moved our mother to an area on a lower floor to allow my sister time to get her hospital bed and equipment moved from my home to hers.

On Sunday, my sister was at the hospital visiting her. She called me in the afternoon and told me to come to the hospital because mother's eyes were fixed and she believed she was passing. My sister had to go to work so she had left by the time I got there. I walked in the room and began to pray. My sister had walked back into the room and interrupted me. I do believe that the interruption was from God and He did not want me to interfere with the process. My sister left to go to work and I stayed in the room with our mother. There was a small bed in the room. I laid down and I felt such a heaviness come upon me that I drifted off to sleep. I would open my eyes to see that my mother was still there alive, then I would doze back off to sleep. I felt as if I was drugged and I couldn't wake myself up. Whatever was going on was between God and my mother, and it was sacred.

IN HIM

Every breath I breathe is the breath You breathe in me
You give me life, refreshed and new
As I come near Your throne
The love You gave to me, I give it back to You Lord
And You give it back to me again
It grows and grows and grows
Until Your love, O God, overtakes me
There's no end to Your love
Your love, O God, completes me and I am whole
My heart is captured by Your heart
You step into my spirit and soul and we become one
I want to stay in Your arms forevermore
Where I am safe and where love is perfect
Where my heart beats with the beat of Your heart
And Your blood runs through my veins
When I stand in You, Jesus
We are one
And I am alive forevermore!

CHAPTER 10

TIME TO SAY GOODBYE

Around 3 o'clock in the morning, the nurses came into the room and informed me that my mother was passing. I woke completely up and stood by her bedside. The nurses left me alone with her. I told her that it was okay for her to go, and that I would be okay. I told her that God had something for me to do. I sang songs to her and told her that I loved her. It felt like we were under an invisible covering like a warm blanket.

I was led to turn my Bible to Revelation Chapter 4. I began to read to her: *"After this I looked, and, behold, a door was opened in heaven: and the first voice which I heard was as it were of a trumpet talking with me; which said, Come up hither, and I will show thee things which must be hereafter. And immediately I was in the spirit: and, behold, a throne was set in heaven, and one sat on the throne. And he that sat was to look upon like a jasper and a sardine stone: and there was a rainbow round about the throne, in sight like unto an emerald. And round about the throne were four and twenty seats: and upon the seats I saw four and twenty elders sitting, clothed in white raiment; and they had on their heads crowns of gold. And out of the throne proceeded lightnings and thunderings and voices: and there were seven lamps of fire burning before the throne, which are the seven Spirits of God. And before the throne there was a sea of glass like unto crystal: and in the midst of the throne, and round about the throne, were four beasts full of eyes before and behind. And the first beast was like a lion, and the second beast was like a calf, and the third beast had a face as a man, and the fourth beast was like a flying eagle. And the four beasts had each of them six wings about him; and they were full of eyes within: and they rest not day and night, saying, Holy, holy, holy, LORD God Almighty, which was, and is, and is to come. And when those beasts give glory and honour and thanks to him that sat on the throne, who liveth for ever and ever, the four and twenty elders fall down before him that sat on the throne, and worship him that liveth for ever and ever, and cast their crowns before the throne, saying, Thou art worthy, O Lord, to receive glory and honour and power: for thou hast created all things, and for thy pleasure they are and were created."*

It was then I saw two tears fall from her right eye. She took two breaths and she was gone. I know that it was her spirit and soul departing. I called the nurse to come into the room, and she confirmed her death at 3:33 am. It was Monday, September 4, 1995, Labor Day.

A close friend of mine had called me days earlier and read to me Jeremiah 33:3. *"Call upon Me and I would show you great and mighty things that you know not of."*

The room was so peaceful. I called my brother who lived in San Antonio and told him that mother had passed. He told me that he was awakened because there was this bright light in his room. He thought it was daylight and he got up to get ready for work. I called my sister who was at work to let her know. She said that she wished she would have stayed, but she was okay. I called my husband and my nephew to let them know and they came together to pick me up from the hospital.

As I waited for the funeral home to come and collect her body, my husband and nephew arrived. They were able to spend some time with her. It was then that I realized I had forgotten to call the funeral home to come and get her. When they finally arrived we had to leave the room. The mortician said that it was so peaceful in the room that they didn't want to disturb her. With me having the privilege and honor of watching my mother depart from this world, my fear of death departed with her. I'd never witnessed anything so beautiful in my life. I knew there were angels in the room and that I was not alone. Her light departed from earth, but I knew she was shining in heaven. I was silent all the way home.

CELEBRATION OF LIFE

She heard the Master call her name
"Come up and don't be late!
Across the Jordan River we must go."
Leading her on towards Heaven's gate.
Calling forth a light to leave the earth
No longer can she stay.
She must shine brighter now than ever before
To help others find their way.
Shh, close your eyes, listen close
To the laughter and the cheers.
I hear her singing songs to Jesus
As He draws her ever near.
Feel her arms of love around you
As she dances towards the sky
"One more kiss," I heard her say.
"Look my loved ones, I can fly!"
So let's rejoice together now,
And give praises to our King
Join in the Celebration of Life
And in the song our mother sings.

CHAPTER 11

THE DAY AFTER

It was early Monday morning. My husband left for work and I had gotten the kids off to school. I went into my mother's room to begin to clean up the apparatus that sustained her life.

All of a sudden, something hit my belly and I began to scream and cry. My beloved mother was gone! I felt so alone. It was as if my heart was being ripped out of my chest. My eldest sister called me to discuss funeral arrangements and a church friend of hers was helping her. I was so angry that she would call me as if it was just another day. I hung up on her. It was more than I could handle. My mother-in-law called me and I was weeping uncontrollably. She began to talk to me and to comfort me. I can't remember a word she said that day, but her words helped me.

When I got off of the phone, the Holy Spirit began to minister and to comfort me. He told me that I had to release my mother. He explained to me that the spiritual soul tie or spiritual umbilical cord was being cut. I had to let her go. It all made sense, but it was still difficult. I was the baby in the family. I was the youngest. I was always the strong one. I was always the one everyone would call when they needed help. At that moment, I wanted to be the needy one. I wanted to be the baby. I didn't want to face this reality. I didn't know how to let her go. My mother was my best friend.

When my two sisters came around, they were arguing about everything in regards to her funeral. After I was alone, the Holy Spirit spoke to me and said, "*Do you see what will happen to your family if you don't take care of this and do what is necessary?*" So much for my pity party. I've come to believe that God provides at least one lamb per each household and family. I believe I was the lamb, and as much as I wanted to be the baby in the family, I could not disobey God.

I called the funeral director at his home that evening. I began to tell him about my day and how my family was falling apart. We discussed what we had to do. God had given me great favor with this man. He was very supportive and kind. At that moment, he was like a big brother to me and it gave me strength. He was the voice of reason. He walked me through the process. My oldest sister and I had done a pre-need contract in preparation of when the time came for us to have to bury our mother. The policy was paid for and we had chosen her casket prior to her passing, but God changed practically everything.

The funeral director offered me a different casket. He only had one left and it was called "The Rose." He said that it would be the perfect casket for my mother. It was beautiful. Early the next morning, my sisters and I came together at my eldest sister's home. Before we began any discussions, I suggested that we pray. We held our hands together as I began to pray and thanked God for our Mother's life. With tears of compassion we asked Him for His guidance. I could feel the atmosphere change. He was with us. My sisters and I began to love on each other, and the Holy Spirit began to guide us.

We had to present a dress to the funeral home. I told my sisters about the rose casket he had offered us. When our parents had remarried, our mother wore a pink dress with a laced V-shaped collar. My sister had borrowed it for her daughter's prom. She had not returned it to our mother, but had it cleaned after the prom. It was hanging in her closet with a plastic covering. It was the perfect dress. None of us could have imagined that her wedding dress would be her "Celebration of Life" dress. We all quickly agreed.

Our eldest sister had to go to work, so my other sister and I went to my house to start making plans. We decided to have the funeral on the following Saturday to allow time for our family to arrive.

The two of us went shopping at the mall. We had one of her pictures enlarged. We found this beautiful 8 x 11 antique gold frame with roses and leaves around it. We went to Foley's department store and found some pearl earrings shaped like teardrops. Our mother's favorite color was red. Our eldest sister was conditioned to wear black for mourning, but the two of us decided to wear red. We bought red and black bracelets for each of us and our sister-in-law, so we could be in unison. Our mother would always tell us to give her flowers while she was alive. Roses were her favorite, however, we instructed others to not buy roses. All of her flowers at her service were carnations.

My sister and I coordinated the program together. My sister wrote out the obituary and she found a written poem from us to her. When we went to the funeral home, I sat in the parlor to write a poem from our mother to us. We presented it to the funeral director, and he had someone to print them. We had so much fun spending time together and planning our mother's Celebration of Life.

I asked my mother's nurse to come to our home and make up her bed. She was excited to do so, and honored that she was included. That was her way of paying tribute to her favorite patient. I had placed petals on the floor. The room was illuminated with the sunlight shining through the windows. When people came to the house, they would stand in the hall and look into the room. Her room was left undisturbed. At first glance my brother was angry because he thought I was making a memorial for her. I explained to him that I did not want the children to be afraid of that room when they came into my home. They would look into the room while our home was full of laughter and love. Only by the grace of God.

I attended church on Wednesday night. Everyone there knew how much I loved and cared for my mother. There was another member whose son passed away the same night as my mom. The pastor called us both to the front and announced that we had lost our loved ones. I told him, "No, I didn't. She's not lost. I know exactly where she is."

The choir began to play some soft music and the pastor stopped them to instruct them to sing songs of praise. My God! We had a beautiful celebration that evening. It was as if all of heaven was celebrating our loved ones.

Her wake was held on Friday evening. I arrived late on purpose. I felt that God was leading me to give my family time to grieve. I had spent every day with her when I brought her into our home. God had me in a place of peace and joy that I didn't think they would understand why I wasn't grieving, so I stayed behind to spend time with God in prayer and fasting. I was full of the joy of the Lord. I had so much peace that it was indescribable.

When my husband and I arrived at the wake the room was filled with laughter, joy and a whole lot of love. Only God can do that. I give Him praise even now for what He did for us.

After the wake was over, my dad's sister had invited us all to her house for dinner. My husband and I did not go. I wanted to rest and spend time in prayer and fasting. When the kids and their cousins came to our house afterwards, there was a line formed in the hallway for the restroom. Something they had eaten gave them diarrhea. We laughed so hard. It was so funny.

The service was on Saturday morning. I was praising and worshiping God all morning until I saw the hearse arrive at my house. I began to weep uncontrollably. One of my church friends pulled up to be part of the procession. I was standing in the middle of the street when she walked up to me and embraced me. I'm certain that she was praying. I think what triggered my emotions was that the hearse was black. It seemed so final. I felt so empty. But, I felt God's love when she wrapped her arms around me. It was as if God Himself was holding me. When I stopped weeping, the joy returned, and I felt such peace and comfort.

When we arrived at the church, I knew that angels were encamped around me and that the Love of God was with me. Everyone was expecting me to cry at the service, but instead, I lifted my hands toward heaven and began to praise and worship God. For the first time, I understood why my mother did that when her mother died. Others said to me that they wanted to cry, but I did not give them permission to do so.

The service was truly a Celebration of Life. The pastor said that the service went longer than most, but he could tell that this woman was special and that she had impacted the lives of many. The church was full of family and friends.

When we arrived at the burial site, the pastor performed the last rites. As we all departed, not one single flower was disturbed. I was accustomed to people taking flowers away with them at funerals, but it just all seemed befitting and honoring her that her flowers remained with her. The sky began to drop rain. I had always heard that was a sign of a person being welcomed home.

Sunday, at church, the brother of the man who passed on the same day as our mother presented me with a white carnation, and told me his brother said to give it to me. I took it home and laid it across her bed.

As I am writing this, just in this moment, I realized that the church where my mother's service was held was close to where I was raped. Eighteen years and nine months later, He still allowed me to hear His voice. Twenty seven years beyond that, He has never left me nor forsaken me and He is alive within me even now. I LOVE YOU, LORD JESUS!!!

I truly must take this moment to pause, and let you know that God is forever with you through the good times and bad times. There is never anything hidden from God. He is the Great I AM and the lifter of our heads!!!! Trust Him with your whole heart because He will not abandon you or I. To God be the Glory for all the marvelous things you have done!!!!

Later on that Sunday evening, I went to the freezer, grabbed my pint of butter pecan ice cream I'd been saving just for this moment, and I went outside. I climbed onto the back of my husband's truck and looked up into this beautiful star filled sky. I talked to God, thanking Him for my mother, my best friend, while enjoying my ice cream.

JESUS, YOU'RE THE SONG IN ME

Every life is an instrument
Every voice is a key
Every heart is a melody
Jesus, You're the song in me
When I gaze across the early morning sky
The evening stars begin to disappear
As I see the sun begin to rise
I feel You near
It's in the quiet of the break of day
When, by Your Spirit, I begin to pray
Lord, my heart is filled with worship and praise
Jesus, You're the song in me
The winds softly whisper to the trees
And they begin to tell Your story
The birds are singing in harmony
As You fill the earth with Your glory
Every life is an instrument of praise
Every voice is a key
Every heart has a song
Jesus, You're the song in me.

CHAPTER 12

OPEN DOORS

The days ahead were not easy. I missed my mother so much that it began to leave a void within my heart. I still had to keep moving. My family needed me, so I had to be strong for them.

One day, feeling totally drained and exhausted, I went to lay down. As soon as my head hit the pillow and I closed my eyes, I saw her. She was standing in a beautiful green field. She looked at me and smiled. She was wearing a white hat. My mother loved hats. All I remember is, "I was awake when I saw her."

I don't know if I fell asleep or if I had left the planet. I do know that when I opened my eyes four hours later, I woke up with so much peace. The grief was gone. I couldn't remember anything else except seeing her in that field. I felt as though God had allowed me to spend that time with her. The children had been so orderly and they did not disturb me. I was not one who would sleep during the day. I knew, without a doubt, that my mother was okay. I was assured that God had a plan for my life.

One day while reading my Bible, I received a call from a friend. She told me that Southwest Airlines was doing interviews at the hotel which was about 5 – 10 minutes from my home. The Holy Spirit spoke to me and told me to go. I had to hurry up and get dressed because the interviews would be over soon. As I was en route, I was feeling that I really wasn't ready to connect back in the world. I was so unprepared. I asked God, "If it's for me, open the door. If it's not, close the door."

I really wasn't looking for a job. I was content being at home. The interviews were ending at 5pm. I arrived around 4:30pm. I didn't have time to complete the application because I was totally unprepared. This lady looked at my application and asked me to come into the call center for a second interview. She gave me the information, and by that day, I was properly prepared.

When I went for the second interview, I was instructed where to go for a drug test. Upon the results of the drug test, she had given me the instructions for training class, and materials to begin studying. I would receive a call. It happened all of a sudden.

Now, my first born son was a senior in high school at the time. When he went to take his SAT exam, I instructed him to fast candy and sweets for the day and to trust God. My kitchen was where I would hear God.

I need to interject here to explain what I'm talking about. When my brother was in the rehab center, there were four homeless men who lived on the sidewalk across from the center. One day after work, I was in the kitchen cooking dinner for my family who hadn't arrived home yet. I heard this **loud voice** speak to me. It had no sound, but the voice was loud. It caused me to tremble on the inside. I heard Him call me by name, "Valerie, if you love me, feed my sheep."

This transpired before I ever went to AZUSA. This happened before I was filled with the Holy Spirit. His voice was audible. He wasn't speaking in my thoughts. He was speaking in my heart. At this time, I didn't understand what He was saying because I didn't know His word. He said it three times.

Later I discovered that He spoke those words to Peter, his disciple. It scared me so much that I started cooking and taking the food downtown to give it to those homeless men. I wouldn't even speak to them. I can only imagine that God must have been shaking His head because I was so naive. I also imagine that He must have been laughing, as well. I believe God has a sense of humor. After I had delivered food to these men a couple of times, they were moved somewhere else. They were no longer on the sidewalk across from the rehab center. Whenever I'm troubled or I can't seem to break through and I really need to hear God's voice for His guidance and instruction, I go to my kitchen.

My son followed the instructions and he did well on the test. I was praying for him, as well. He had not applied for any colleges, but God reminded me what He did for me when I graduated from high school. I went to school for a summer program and received a scholarship where I did not have to pay a dime for tuition.

One day at his school, there were some recruiters from Drexel University in Philadelphia. They were in the hallway and they asked my son if he would like a scholarship to attend their school. We had never heard of that university. He asked them if his friend could receive a scholarship as well, and they said yes. His friend decided he didn't want to go to Drexel, but only God could do something like that. My son would only have to pay for his books and his transportation.

My brother lived in Virginia, which wasn't too far from where the university was. It was about an hour and a half away from my brother's home. I had no idea how he was going to get there, though. I did not realize that God was opening doors.

I was in the training class at Southwest Airlines one evening and everyone had left the room for their break. Alone in that room I began to cry and pray and was feeling a bit overwhelmed. I wasn't ready to go back to work. I just didn't know how my son was going to get back and forth to Philadelphia. My response was, "Southwest Airlines does not fly into Philadelphia," as if God didn't know that already. And I heard Him say, but they will one day. In the meantime, he would be able to fly to Baltimore. My brother was there to take care of him and get him to school. God had opened the door. All I needed to do was to trust Him and walk through the door. Needless to say, I passed the class and was hired on as a part time employee.

That's what I needed because I had three children at home who were still in school. I had free flight benefits and so did my husband and my children. He followed in my footsteps and majored in engineering. During his difficult times I told him he could change his major, but he refused. I was and still am very proud of him. He pursued his dream and has prospered in it, as well.

Mind you, I was praying that Southwest would start flying to Philadelphia. There is a lesson in that. They did begin to service Philadelphia, but only after he had graduated. He worked during the summer in Houston the year before and was able to buy his first car. He would drive from Houston to Virginia. I would go with him because it was basically a twenty three hour drive nonstop. We would take turns driving. We would spend the night at my brother's house and he would continue the drive to school. My brother would take me to Dulles Airport which was fifteen minutes from his house and I would fly back home to Houston. God makes a way - God is the way.

One thing we were told at SWA was that we couldn't talk about religion on the phone. This was a business. I could hear God's voice tell me that He was my source. I received calls from people who were looking for more than a flight. They needed help. On occasion, I was able to encourage people on the line and give them hope. There were those who were sick in their bodies and some were facing real challenges in life. I'd tell them what God can and will do. I kept little inspiration booklets on healing and I would send it to them. I would pray for people, and at times, I would send them a poem I had written to encourage them. They would be inspirational and full of hope. I would receive back wonderful letters and beautiful cards, thanking me and sharing their testimonies of what God had done for them.

I remember this one incident where a lady's husband had been in a wreck in another state and she was trying to go and see him. He was a truck driver and he was taken to the hospital. A last minute ticket was extremely high and she couldn't afford it. I took a break and called her back. I told her I would give her one of my buddy passes so she could go and be with her husband. We set up a meeting place where I gave her a pass and instructions on what she had to do.

She couldn't believe that a total stranger would bless her and not take anything from her, but God was my boss and He gets the glory. He opened the door for her. Not only was I able to help people in difficult situations, I was also able to help employees, friends, and family, as well. One evening, this man called my line and he was speaking foul and lustful words on the line. We received those calls rather often as well. Generally, we would just hang up. As he was talking, I began to talk to him and ask him who had hurt him so badly. I began to tell him about God. He started sharing his pain and he began to weep. He apologized to me. God opened the door for him.

I remember this call I received from a grandmother who was having to raise her grandchildren. I was in tears when the call ended. I began to tell God that I wanted to be able to help grandmothers who had to raise their grandchildren, as well as mothers who were struggling to raise their children alone. Drugs were infiltrating homes and ripping families apart. Babies were being born with drugs in their system. Families were being torn apart and they needed to be healed.

I had a friend at church whose husband left her for another woman. They had a teenage daughter and a teenage son who was confined to a wheelchair. Her husband left her for another woman, and she had to care for her children alone. I never saw her complain. She was in her early 40's when she suddenly passed away. She was a beautiful woman inside and out. She took care of her children and she served in the church. She loved God with all her heart. Her daughter married shortly after and her son went to live with his dad. Even when you don't know how or why, God opens doors. God makes a way when it seems there is no way.

LIFE

A smile, a simple act of kindness
Can help someone today
Joy is not found in what you get
But in what you give away
The softest touch, the kindest word
Can heal a wounded soul
Love that says, "I understand"
Is worth its weight in gold
Life will teach you many things
Concerning matters of the heart
But remember to submit them all in prayer
And God will do His part
Love will yield its greatest fruit
In what you do and say
Love will bear all things and hope all things
As you live life day to day.

CHAPTER 13

DIVINE CONNECTIONS

One night, I received a call from a minister in Detroit, Michigan. She called to get a flight to California. As I was talking to her, I heard God say, "Take down her phone number." I jotted down her phone number. Then, she said to me, "Valerie, I need you to take down my phone number. I need to talk to you away from work."

She indicated that she was a Prophetess and she had a word from God for me. It took me a little time to convince myself to call her.

Three days later I mustered up the courage to call. Before I did, though, I prayed and asked God that if this was truly Him, to have her pray before she started talking to me. I picked up the phone and dialed her number. She answered. Not only did she answer, she remembered me. And then she said, "I can tell you what God is saying, but I feel led to pray first."

I was convinced it was God. This woman spoke to me concerning my past, my present and my future. I had never had a close encounter with a Prophet before. She spoke for an hour nonstop and I was taking notes. She was exact when she spoke of my past and I knew she was a woman of God. It scared me so that someone I had never met would tell me so much about me. She spoke about pain in my life. She gave me instructions and I was to call her back.

It took me two weeks to build up the courage to call her back. She then invited me to come to Detroit. She was ministering at a church and so I went. I flew for free with my benefits and she put me up in this really nice hotel. She poured into me and showered me with gifts. Nobody in my life had ever shown me such love.

She didn't even know me. She ministered to me. On top of that, she paid for an extra day for me to stay.

I had gone to ministries where I had witnessed people being healed. In the church I attended, I had witnessed people being filled with the Holy Spirit and I saw people healed. I had not witnessed a prophetic ministry of this magnitude. I had never been that close to a man or woman of God before who operated with that gift. She introduced me to God in a way I had never known Him to be, and she poured into my life. She taught me things that I did not know. When she traveled as a minister, I was able to travel with her. God had not only made a way for my son to go to school out of state, he provided a way for me to travel and train under a great teacher and mentor.

Not too long after I had met the Prophetess, I received a call at work from a lady pastor in Ohio. She was making a reservation to visit her family. She was going through something at that time. Through a phone call, I introduced her to my mentor. We all came together and became friends. This was a divine connection by God. We were a threesome and would meet up in places for ministry. God placed not one, but two dynamic women in my life who would teach me, pray for and with me, and most of all, love me – the imperfect flawed me.

Every time I boarded a plane to go meet them, I would go through healing and deliverance. I would always return home feeling closer to God and His Love. Where I used to feel I was alone, God gave me divine connections with people I could trust and believe they truly loved me. I've learned so much from them. I am still learning from them. We would worship together, pray together and talk about God. Oh, yes, they would correct me when I was wrong, as well! That's love. God corrects those whom He loves, and I've grown a lot. God connected them to me so that I could grow into His calling and His purpose.

I have learned and believe we all must be accountable and teachable. We need each other. Growing pains hurt sometimes, but our lives can be fruitful and wonderful, as well. They have loved me through the good, the bad, and the ugly. We remain connected through the love of God. They are busy serving God in full time ministry.

However, we still pray together. We still worship together. We still do ministry together. We laugh and cry together, and we love each other. We are truly a part of God's family. I've heard it said that sometimes people are in your life for a season or sometimes for a lifetime. God was truly moving in my life.

One of the ministers who was in the same church I attended had left the church and started his ministry. Within his ministry, he also had a school of ministry. He and the pastor were close friends, as well. The pastor asked the senior pastor's permission to allow me to help him in his ministry and to attend his school of ministry. It was a long drive for me, but I was still hungry and following God's plan. He was a great teacher of God's word. Within a year, the classes covered the Bible. This pastor gave me the opportunity to teach and preach. He would visit other countries for ministry and he would practically leave me in charge. I know it was God.

I was in charge of the Women's Ministry. I was the Sunday School teacher, and I was allowed to preach the word when the pastor was unavailable. I also had a key to the building. I was the first person to arrive to make sure everything was set up properly and that everything was clean. I cleaned the toilets too. God was taking me to another level in Him. I also began leading prayer conferences at this church. I was in training. God was raising me up. He gave me such favor. It wasn't easy. I had to become disciplined in the things of God and overcome adversities. No matter what, I depended on God and I trusted Him.

The first prayer conference God gave me, my friends from Detroit and Ohio came to support me and to minister. Most of the people who came were from different churches. The people who attended that church did not attend. I didn't understand it at the time, but I do now. I poured out everything I had to give, and unfortunately, there were a few people there who were not pleased with me because of the favor of God that was upon my life. I still loved them and served them while I was there. More than likely, it was a test I had to pass. God was preparing me and allowing me to see that not everyone would be on my side.

I had to learn to endure hardships. I had completed the lessons from this school of ministry, and God opened the door for me to attend The School of the Prophets. It was once a week and the pastor I was serving at the time did not approve. It did not conflict with any of my obligations to the church. The pastor turned against me, but I knew the voice of God and He was the one who opened the door.

I still served the church with my whole heart. I went through some persecution, but I kept praying, kept serving and I learned so much. Although I felt as though they turned on me, I continued to be faithful to God and to the church. Yes, it hurt, but I still walked in love and forgiveness and I took whatever was given to me. I went where God sent me. I had already felt the anointing for me to be there was lifted, and God was leading me elsewhere. I still served the church and God as I always did.

One Sunday, I spoke with the pastor to let him know that my season was up. He told me that he didn't want me there anyway. He spoke some horrible things to me and about me. He said he was glad I was leaving. I heard in my heart that it was a test. I remained calm and simply agreed with him and asked him to pray for me.

I think he was shocked at the way I responded. I let him know that I loved him and the church, and I left gracefully. I was excited that I passed the test. Matthew 5:25 says to agree with your adversary quickly while you are on the way with him, lest your adversary deliver you to the judge, the judge hands you over to the officer and you be thrown into prison. I had spent months in prayer, so after he spoke to me so unkindly, those words would try to haunt me and hurt me. I went before God in prayer. I wanted to know how God felt because I didn't want to disappoint God.

When I went before God all I felt was God's love. I never did tell my husband what I had experienced. I didn't want him to be upset. I realized that it was God who closed the door because He had something else for me. I really had stayed beyond my time, but I wanted to make sure it was God and not me. I returned to the church that I so loved and was well received. I was sitting on the back row of the church when the pastor called me up to pray. I was welcomed with open arms.

NOT ME

When I look into the eyes of another
And they look back at me
Let it not be my eyes, Lord
But Yours they see
When I speak into the life of another
Let it not be my voice that's near
But let it be Your voice they hear
When I reach out to touch someone
Whose heart is still and cold
Let it be Your touch, Lord
That heals the wounded soul
When Your Spirit flows through me
Lord, let Your love consume me
When I stand before Your people Lord
Let it be You they see
.....Not me.

CHAPTER 14

HEALING CHURCH HURT

I was glad to be back at my home church with my church family. When I had the first prayer conference at the other church both the pastor and the youth pastor came. The youth pastor was one of my speakers and the pastor came to support us. I believe he saw the growth in me. He asked me about the Prophetess, my mentor. He said that he saw a huge light beaming on her head while she was ministering.

This man was, and is, like a spiritual father to me. I have received so much healing and love through him. I had made a vow to plant $1000 to the church. I didn't have it at the time, but I was trusting God for it. The bible says that He gives seed to the sower and bread to the eater. I was able to fulfill that vow. God had instructed me to take my check to the church and put it in his hand.

I went to the church and I actually attempted to just drop it in the box. The front door was locked, so I could not enter. I had to enter the door by the offices. He wasn't there. He came in right after I had entered. When I saw him he really wasn't in the mood to be bothered by anyone. I told him I just came by to bring him something and I handed him the check. When he saw it, he invited me into his office. He began to weep. He told me that the church needed a breakthrough and he had been praying to God to fulfill the financial need. He also told me that the woman who was the prayer coordinator of the church had left. He asked me if I would take it over. I asked him if I could pray about it, and if I could go into the Sanctuary to pray.

Sadly, through the years, I had experienced quite a bit of hurt from the church. I had gone through a lot of hurt in my life already. I was talked about, lied on, made fun of, and isolated at times by leaders and members of the church. I refer to them as church cliques. They would talk about each other, as well. When I opened my eyes to see and my heart to understand, I drew away from them. I would still serve and help out for the most part. If it wasn't about God, I wasn't a part of it. I was so focused on serving, loving God and loving people. I didn't know that church people could be so cruel.

I wasn't the only one. I was so willing to serve that at one point, I realized I was being taken advantage of. There wasn't anything I would not do for God or for people. I wasn't polished. I didn't have expensive clothes. My nails weren't polished. I wasn't groomed like they were. I was broken. They didn't know my life. They didn't know I was going through depression and was struggling to take care of my family. They didn't know that I would cry myself to sleep at night. I was a plain, simple person who could easily be lost in a crowd.

I kept coming. I kept serving. I wanted to be part of something, but I simply did not like cliques. Once I saw their hearts, I backed away from them. I loved them and I gleaned from their teachings, but I was a misfit among them. I felt like I grew alone, but it was nothing new to me. There were some people who saw me for me and I felt safe with them. They were talked about too, but they truly loved God. So basically, I was associated with the misfits. I'm not saying this to judge or criticize, but everything that's shiny on the outside does not sparkle. Everything is not as it appears to be.

At the church I had just left, someone had a picture of me on the bulletin board. I hadn't even seen it.

My baby girl saw that someone had put pins all in the picture. She was so hurt. We were in service where I was standing before the church, and I asked the question, why would anyone do something like that. I did nothing to deserve it. The pastor took the picture out of my hand and began to address the congregation. Those who were involved came to me and apologized. I knew that it was because they were exposed and their words were not genuine. Their hearts had not changed towards me. These were leaders as well, who would contaminate the sheep. The Bible says to beware of wolves in sheep's clothing. I suppose this was a lesson I had to learn. I've grown wiser and more compassionate because of those experiences. They were part of my growth.

One morning, while I'm sitting in the back of church, enjoying the presence of God, I heard in my spirit to go and make peace with those who hurt you. God, really? I thought I was done with those people. Matthew 5:23-24 says, *"Therefore if you bring your gift to the altar, and there remember that your brother has something against you, leave your gift there before the altar, and go your way. First be reconciled to your brother, and then come and offer your gift."*

Some of the women who had hurt me were no longer in this church. I had to find out where they were, go, and apologize to them. I asked them to forgive me if I had offended them or hurt them in any way. At the time I did not understand why God had me to do this because I didn't treat anyone badly or put anyone down. I understood the hurt and pain, the rejection, and not fitting in. But, I did what God told me to do. It wasn't for them. It was for me. God was healing me. He was cleansing me. He was freeing me. He was elevating me. I obeyed His instruction and I felt free. It freed me and enlarged my capacity to love even more.

When I took on the responsibility of ministering to the women at the church I had just left, I didn't feel qualified. When I was asked to do it, I spent time reading God's word and I began to weep. I told God that I did not know enough about His word. I felt so unprepared and unworthy for the task. I heard Him say, "Life has taught you. I started teaching you as a little girl. You are not alone. I am with you."

The very first time I stood before those women, they did not respond well to me at all. I went back to God and asked Him, "What should I do?"

He told me to wash their feet. There was also a woman in my life who was older than I. God had her teach me, pray with me, correct me, and help me. She would come to assist me with these women until the pastor drove her away. So, at the following meeting, I humbled myself and washed their feet. I prayed for each of them as I knelt before them. I wept. They wept. We all felt the presence of God. Most of the women there were from a different culture and country.

God broke all of us that day and we had some awesome times with God during our meetings. It profits you to obey God's instructions. As I went to the people to be reconciled, the love of God healed my heart. The journey I had traveled was leading me to a destiny in God. I was equipped to help people. I had prayed, "God, teach me to love like You love."

I didn't realize that it would come with persecution and pain, but I truly love people and I have compassion for people who are hurting. After I had obeyed God, I accepted the position from the pastor. He didn't announce it right away because there were others who wanted to head up the prayer. I would come to the Sanctuary every Tuesday morning at 10am with the woman who stood with me when I led the Women's Ministry at

---

the other church. She was also a member of this church. We would pray. It was a time of intercession and preparation for what was to come. God was truly moving in the church and in our lives.

The pastor had invited the intercessors out for dinner to make his announcement. There were some who were not pleased with his decision. I knew it was God, though. He had opened the door. He had trained me and equipped me. Some of the people were loyal to the woman who left. I didn't let that affect me because God was my boss. God had given me some instructions, and on a Saturday, I had my first meeting with the intercessors. There were some who quit the prayer ministry and there were others who embraced it. They had to get to know me. They had to get to know the God in me. We still had prayer every day of the week.

On Saturdays we all met together. I taught them the way God led me. As I was trained, I began to train them, so that we would all be on one accord. One of the requirements was that before they could go to the altar to pray for others, we had to come together and pray together. Spiritually, I wanted them to be protected. They knew the guidelines and God truly was with us. We saw God do some wonderful things and the services were awesome. He showed up and people grew in God.

We had fun, as well. I would give them assignments and they would have to bring a message and teach. I was preparing them to be leaders. One of the prayer meetings did not have many people in attendance, but the meetings began to grow. I was allowed to do prayer conferences here, as well. The first one I did here, I invited the pastor from the other church to be a keynote speaker. He declined at the last minute. I had to stand in. The message was "*My House Shall Be A*

House Of Prayer For All Nations." God was truly with me.

One morning, that pastor was visiting the church and he was praying for people at the altar. I was actually happy to see him. I went to him to greet him and I told him that I loved him. He said something harsh and ugly to me, but it was not my issue. It was his. He actually called me one day on the phone to apologize. I know that was God's doing. We haven't spoken since, but when he comes across my heart, I pray for him. God has joined me with wonderful people to serve with.

Some years later, the pastor of the church was ill and he moved to another state. He was truly a spiritual father to me and so many others. His name was Love. The church was assigned to some new pastors. My service there was up, so it was time for me to move again. Some of those wonderful people are still in my life. They are still in love with God and serving God.

However, God opened another door for me. I've had the privilege and honor of serving other ministries. I've had a key to nearly every church God has placed me. For thirteen years, God had assigned me to have Prayer Summits. We would have one night of consecration and one to two days of ministry and prayer. I had begun to seek God for months for direction. I fasted and prayed. I began to ask God, "Where is my spiritual father?"

I felt an emptiness within me. I knew I was in transition, but I just didn't know what God was up to. I stayed at home for about a month studying His word and seeking His face.

One Sunday, my daughter invited me to go to this church with her. We were sitting in the back of the church when the pastor called for me to stand up. He began to give me a prophetic word telling me that in seven days I would be in a new place. God was answering my prayer. I did not have a clue what he meant. During the week, one of my friends from Pastor Love's church told me that he would be ministering at a church in Clear Lake on that Sunday. God had given me an answer.

Sunday morning, my daughters and I were there, bright and early. When we walked through the door, he literally called out my name. We both were so excited. God had healed him and sent him back. The presence of God was so strong in the building.

Later, he called me on the phone. I have no idea how he got my number because I had not given it out. On the following Sunday, he asked if I would teach the adult Sunday School. God opened yet another door. Soon afterwards, he met me in the hallway and told me that my class was truly a ministry. People would come to the class, and afterwards, there would be someone lingering wanting to talk to me and asking me for prayer.

I had to keep tissues in my classroom. People would be weeping. The woman who was over the Sunday School department would weep often. God was with me. My sister who was seven years older than me wasn't feeling well. Her bank where she worked was taken over by another bank, and she was about to be let go. She had worked there for most of her adult years as an accountant, but the other bank was bringing in their own staff. She thought she was experiencing depression. When she went to the doctor, she was diagnosed with depression and was being treated for that.

One day, I went to see her and she was in pain. I made an appointment for her with my primary doctor and she was seen right away. My sister was about to lose her benefits because her job was ending and the doctor moved quickly to set up appointments with specialists. She underwent several tests. Myself and her youngest daughter were with her when she went to the chief surgeon for the results. He told her she had stage four cancer with about three months to live. When we got to the elevator, she broke down and began to cry. I told her, "We know somebody. You are in a win-win situation. If God heals you, you win. If God decides to take you home, you win. So, we fight."

I was on my way to her house one morning, weeping and crying out to God, "What shall I do?"

He spoke to my heart and said, "No greater love has a man than this, that he lay down his life for his friend."

She was one of my very best friends who was always there for me. I spoke to the pastor and told him about my sister. I resigned from teaching Sunday School to care for my sister. The surgeon said she had probably three months to live. When we spoke to the oncologist, he was asked the same question. His response was, that's between you and God. Within a week she was receiving chemotherapy treatments.

We spent practically every day together. She had some rough days, but we had fun. We would sing, laugh, go out to eat, go shopping, go to the movies, and whatever she wanted to do, we did.

Some days, she could not get out of bed. Our eldest sister, the nurse, was helping at first, but soon it was just she and I. Her eldest daughter worked during the week. Her youngest daughter was a captain in the Army and she was out of the country on duty. For Christmas, her daughter was finished with her tour. It had been a year since my sister was given three months to live. She decorated the house. She and her daughter cooked. I think I slept most of the day. I was tired and she was full of energy.

A year and almost eight months later after she received the diagnosis, she passed away. When she started this journey her cancer count was 10,000. She had some sort of bowel obstruction and had to have surgery. At this point, her cancer count was 3. When she had the surgery, the cancer began to spread. The surgeon gave her a week to live. It was in June.

She passed away six days before her 65th birthday on August 16th. It's not over until God says it's over. She didn't want a funeral. She wanted us to gather together and have Thanksgiving. Her daughters honored her request. They had a celebration at her house with family and her friends. To be absent from the body is to be present with the Lord. We celebrated her life and she celebrated her birthday in the presence of God. She won.

SHE'S FREE

God opened His hands to let her fly
He set her free against the sky
She soars the heavens through clouds way high
She's free, she's free, she's free.

She touched the hearts of yours and mine
There's sorrow in those she left behind
On the wings of God's love, the higher she climbs
She's free, she's free, she's free.

Life goes on for those of us
Who learned to love her so very much
There are no more tears for her to shed
No more pain, nor hung down head
She's entered into eternity
She's free! She's Free! She's FREE!

CHAPTER 15

LOVE IS THE KEY

From the rejection of the womb all the way to my last breath, I would not trade anything for my journey. Just to know that God was, and is, always with me gives me the strength and hope for a brighter day. To have a relationship with God is personal. Who can fathom the depth of the Father's love? He loved us so much that He sacrificed His only begotten son to die for the whole world.

I have lived through so much pain and disappointment, and yet, today I rejoice over every trial and test which has navigated me to where I am right now. No one enjoys hurt, pain or loss. It is never easy to endure heartache, abuse, and disappointments. Suffering is not fun, but no one has to suffer in silence. Not only did I hear God's voice, He heard mine. Just to know that we are never alone, and that God's love never fails, gives me hope and peace and strength to carry on. I have learned to take the things that the devil has meant for my demise and use it for good. I have learned so much about God and myself. I am still learning. God has cleansed me from the inside out and given me joy unspeakable and full of His glory. Jesus Christ, His only begotten son has paid the cost for our redemption with His very own blood so that we might be free.

There are so many people who have gone through and are going through trauma, hurt, pain, disappointments, sickness, disease, heartache – all sorts of things. One of the lessons I have learned is that holding onto those things is not a way to live. We have to let go and give it to God. God is the way through. He's the way out. He is the way to everything we need or desire. He makes a way when there seems to be no way. He is the way to life itself. He is the light which shines and guides us through the darkness of our lives. He has given us the keys to open doors. He walks with us. He guides us. He communes with us. He teaches us. His Spirit will abide with us if we let Him. He's our Creator, our Redeemer, Our Heavenly Father, and He is my very best friend. God is Love. We are never alone and He will never abandon us.

I believe that the things that I've gone through have shaped me into who I am today... He's not finished with me, yet. I used to be bitter, but now I am a better person, a better wife, a better mother, a better friend and a better servant. In my journey with God, I've learned how to forgive others, how to forgive myself and how to forgive God. He has poured so much love into me that I have not only fallen in love with God, I have fallen in love with people and I love myself.

The world would be such a better place if we all would turn to God and embrace His love. If we would learn His ways and hear His voice, our lives would be richer, our joy would be greater. Our compassion for others would be greater. Watching the news where I see the suffering and pain of others breaks my heart. I pray each and every day for every soul, every person on this planet because, whether good or bad, we are all God's children. Our fights and our battles are not with one another. We wrestle not against flesh and blood, but against powers, principalities and rulers in high places. There's a constant battle going on and it is good versus evil, righteousness versus ungodliness, the kingdom of God versus the kingdom of darkness whose ruler is the devil. Just as there is day and night, light and darkness, there is good and evil.

Looking back over my life, I realize just how blessed I am. I have family, I have friends, I have forgiveness, and most of all, I have the Spirit of the Living God dwelling on the inside of me. There is a place in God's heart for all of us. I believe the more we love, the more we forgive, the more we serve and look after one another, the more pleased God is because He is LOVE. We must acknowledge Him, commune with Him, take His hand and walk with Him. Receive His love towards us. It takes courage to heal. God is the Healer.

I pray that you receive God's healing and His love. Enjoy the journey. Jeremiah 29:11-12 says, *"For I know the plans I have for you,"* declares the Lord, *"plans to prosper you and not harm you, plans to give you hope and a future. Then you will call on me and come and pray to me, and I will listen to you."*

It is my earnest hope and prayer that you also shall find the courage to heal, and that your life will be the instrument to heal others. Love is the Key. Let your light so shine before men that they may see your good works and glorify our Father in Heaven. Let us run this race with patience and love, and see what the end will be.

With one final thought, as we all go through the process of healing in every area of our lives where there is hurt, pain, disappointments and trials, LET IT GO. Take a deep breath and know that you are inhaling the very breath of God. Then, exhale and let go of all those things which have held you bound and have tried to keep you from your destiny in God. Just LET IT GO. Be your best self, be great, be healed, be free, but never let go of God's hand.

EVERY MORNING WHEN I RISE

Every morning when I rise
I will stand and give You Praise
For You alone are Worthy
And to You my heart I raise
With gratitude and humility
I bow before my King
For in this life I live, Lord,
You're my everything
To serve You is My honor
Though at times the task seems hard
To Worship You is my privilege
To love You is my reward.
So every morning when I rise
I will stand and give You Praise
For You alone are Worthy
And to You my heart I raise.

BE THE LIGHT

Though the days may seem dark
This journey through life may seem long
The path you travel may seem rough
Just know you're never alone
Take hold to the Hand of Faith
Trust and believe that God will see you through
His Love is everlasting
His promises are ever true
Be the Light.

Stay close to your family and friends
Keep them ever so dear to your heart
For there's a light that shines from within
That will guide them through the dark
Hold on to the Hand of Faith
Let God's love shine through you
Show kindness and forgiveness to others
Let them know God loves them too
Be the Light.

Do what is right and pleasing to God
When you're going through trials and tests
Humble yourself before God's Mighty Hand
And He will do the rest
God will fight your battles
As you take hold to the Hand of Faith
Let your light so shine before men
So they too may know His Grace
Be the Light.

TODAY IS THE DAY OF SALVATION

Today is the day of salvation
Today He will set you free
He loves you more than words can say
That's why He died for you and me
He's calling you by name
Our debt – He paid the cost
He died that all the world may live
He wants no one to be lost
He will fill the empty places
He will give you a brand new start
He will prepare a place for you in Heaven
If you invite Him into your heart
Just say this simple prayer
And ask Jesus to come in
To take away your sorrow
And to forgive all your sin
Thank Him and believe Him
That what He says is true
Old things are passed away
And now your life is new
Begin to read the Word of God
And spend time in prayer each day
Call upon His Holy Spirit
And He'll teach you His will and way.

LIFE FOR A LIFE

Who am I, 'O Lord,
That you would consider me your son
Why would You love me so
After all the things I've done
Why would You send your only Son
To die upon a tree
When HE had done no wrong
And it should have been me.

It was grace, It was grace, My son
That I sent to show the way
It was grace, it was My grace
That was the price He would pay
A life for a life
A soul for a soul
He gave His very all
To make you whole.

It was love, it was love, My son
That would save the world from sin
It was love, it was My love
That would bring you back again
A life for a life
A soul for a soul
He gave is His very all
To make you whole.

HE defeated death and the grave
And He gave you the key
He filled you with the Holy Spirit
Now live your life for Me
Go and tell others
Of the price My Son has paid

Tell them of His sacrifice
And how they too can be saved.

Tell them their sins will be forgiven
They will never be alone
He'll never leave them nor forsake them
Since their sins have been atoned
A life for a life
A soul for a soul
He gave His very all
To make you whole.

A life for a life
A soul for a soul
The debt of sin has been paid in full
Now you are whole.

UNIQUELY YOU

My strong beautiful Sista', sometimes navigating through life may be difficult, but you were built for the tasks which lie before you!
You are strong
You are beautiful
You are uniquely you
You are a beacon of light to others
You are laughter
You are powerful
You are greatness
When darkness comes to extinguish your light, your love, your laughter
Don't give in - don't give up
Fight for your joy
Fight for your light because
You are strong
You are powerful
You are uniquely you
When you think you can no longer fight
Take the hand of someone who is Strong
Who is Beautiful
Who is Powerful
And who loves you even in the dark times
We are built for this and l will not let go
So fight to break through the darkness
And come back into the light
Because you are strong
You are beautiful
You are powerful
You are uniquely you.

PRAYER

Heavenly Father, I pray for each and every person who is reading this book. I pray that by sharing my experiences, my life, and my heart, that many will look to You for the way and the answers to their own questions as they go through their own life challenges. I pray that many will take heart and have the courage to heal, forgive, and to love. Father, I pray that You will release healing in every heart, in every home, in every family so that we all may be whole and one in You. May Your anointing destroy every yoke of bondage in the name of Jesus, Yeshua, our Counsellor, our Messiah, our Prince of Peace. May we all draw close to You and to stay close to You. Mend broken hearts and heal wounded souls, Lord. Forgive us of our sins and make our lives brand new. Your mercies are new every morning and Your grace is sufficient for us. Restore us. Heal us. Fill us. Use our lives as instruments of Your peace and Your love. Teach us Your ways, 'O God. Open the windows of Heaven and pour out blessings upon your children. I pray that every heart be healed and every soul be saved. Cover your people with Your glory. Cover the earth with Your glory. I pray that many will be delivered and set free by the Power of Your Name and by the blood of Jesus the Christ, the Son of the Living God. May old things and old ways pass away and may all things become new. Thank you, Father, for loving us so much. Thank you, Jesus, for loving us so very much. Thank you, Holy Spirit, for loving us so much. I love you, Father, and it's in Jesus' name, I pray.

AMEN.

The Chris Young Foundation

FIGHTING TO RESTORE JUSTICE THROUGH

LOVE, FORGIVENESS, & SECOND CHANCES

CHRISYOUNGFOUNDATIONLF2C.ORG